DIRECT HITS

Toughest Vocabulary of the SAT

VOLUME 2

Fourth Edition

For more information, please contact us by mail:

Direct Hits Publishing
2639 Arden Rd., Atlanta GA 30327

Ted@DirectHitsPublishing.com

Or visit our website:
www.DirectHitsPublishing.com

Fourth Edition: December 2011

ISBN: 978-1-936551-06-4

Edited by Ted Griffith
Cover Design by Carlo da Silva
Interior Design by Alison Rayner

ACKNOWLEDGEMENTS

This fourth edition reflects the collaborative efforts of an outstanding team of students, educators, reviewers, and project managers, each one committed to helping young people attain their highest aspirations. Their insights and talents have been incorporated into this latest version of *Direct Hits*.

We wish to express our gratitude to Jay Patel and Mary Catherine Lindsay, who researched, refined, and updated many of the examples used in the books.

We are also grateful to educator Susan Maziar for her valuable insights, gleaned from her tutoring experience and from taking the SAT and ACT, and to Jane Armstrong for her editing and her eloquent wordsmithing.

Alison Rayner was responsible for creating our new interior design. We thank her not only for her creative talent but also for her flexibility through multiple revisions. Additionally, we are grateful to Carlo da Silva, who once again used his artistic and graphic skills to design our distinctive cover.

Jane Saral's extensive experience as an English teacher and writing instructor enhanced our literary content and expertly guided our editing and proof-reading efforts. We thank her for her diligence and patience throughout this process. We will never look at the Oxford Comma the same way again! A big thank you goes out to Luther Griffith for his oversight, ensuring that schedules were adhered to and deadlines were met.

Finally, an extra-special thank you goes to Claire Griffith for her extraordinary work in coordinating and directing the team, compiling the material for the revisions, her creative ideas, and her constant focus on the highest quality content. Without her, this book would not have been possible.

Ted Griffith, *Editor*

TABLE OF CONTENTS

INTRODUCTION

Why is a superior vocabulary important, you ask?

Words are our tools for learning and communicating. A proficient and robust vocabulary is critical to your success in school, business, the professions, and particularly, on the PSAT and SAT. Yet most students agree that memorizing long lists of seemingly random words is a tedious chore.

Like its companion book *Volume 1*, *Direct Hits Toughest Vocabulary of the SAT Volume 2* offers a different approach. Each word is illustrated through relevant examples from popular movies, television, literature, music, historical events, and current headlines. Students can place the words in a context they can easily understand and remember.

For example, you will discover that French King Louis XIV and the American rapper 50 Cent share a PENCHANT for ORNATE decorations while Queen Elizabeth I and Rick "The Big Boss" Ross share a passion for OSTENTATIOUS jewelry. You will also learn about a PRISTINE rain forest, a PROLIFIC NFL scorer, a PERFIDIOUS traitor, and a PARSIMONIOUS miser.

While *Volume 1* covers the core SAT vocabulary, this book tackles 210 of the SAT's **most challenging words**, that often appear in Level 4 and Level 5 questions.

We begin with 60 essential academic terms taken from the disciplines of science, literature, and the social sciences—all words that appear in your textbooks and on the SAT.

Our next chapter defines 22 words that look familiar but actually have multiple meanings. These everyday words such as FLAG, CHECK, and COIN have surprising secondary meanings that can trick unsuspecting students. A high score can depend on your knowing the alternate definitions.

Finally, we take on the SAT's toughest words. Their meanings can be NUANCED in such a way as to ELUDE all but the most DILIGENT students. Without a precise understanding of their definitions, many students will miss the subtle differences between the answer choices.

Building on the success of previous editions, the authors of *Direct Hits Toughest Vocabulary of the SAT* consulted secondary school teachers, tutors, parents, and students from around the world to ensure that these words and illustrations are exactly on target to **further** prepare you for success on the SAT.

Direct Hits offers **selective** vocabulary using **relevant** examples with **vivid** presentation so you can achieve successful **results** on standardized tests and in life.

Let's press on!

CHAPTER 7

Rhetorical/Literary Terms
221 – 235

RHETORIC is the art of using words effectively in both speaking and writing, often in order to influence or persuade others. It is a term often used to describe the art of prose composition, and under its umbrella are many figures of speech.

You might think that **LITERARY** terms such as **METAPHOR**, **ANECDOTE**, and **ALLUSION** are only useful in English class. NOT so. Rhetorical and literary terms show up in many places, even in our everyday lives. In this chapter we explore 15 terms that have frequently turned up on PSAT, SAT, and AP tests. Recognizing them will result in higher scores, but even better, using a variety of **RHETORICAL DEVICES** can enhance your writing and speaking and result in richer, more powerful, more effective expression.

221 | FIGURATIVE/METAPHORICAL LANGUAGE

A general term referring to language that describes a thing in terms of something else. The resemblance is FIGURATIVE, not LITERAL, as the reader is carried beyond the LITERAL meaning to consider the NUANCES (Word 354) and connotations of the words used in the comparison.

METAPHOR can occur as a single comparison or as the central or controlling image of a whole poem or work. For instance:

"Whoso List to Hunt," a sonnet by the English poet Sir Thomas Wyatt (1503-1542), is **LITERALLY** about a man's **FUTILE** (Word 46) pursuit of an elusive deer. But it is usually seen as the tale of his fruitless wooing of an elusive woman, probably Anne Boleyn, who had married Henry VIII. The deer imagery of beauty, daintiness, and quickness **EVOKES** (Word 13) the characteristics of a woman and thus functions as the controlling **METAPHOR** of the poem.

There are many literary terms for different kinds of **NONLITERAL**, **METAPHORICAL**, or **FIGURATIVE** language. Here are several of the most common terms.

222 | SIMILE

An EXPLICIT (clearly stated) figure of speech that is a comparison between two essentially unlike things, usually using the words "like" or "as," which points out a FIGURATIVE way that the two things ARE alike.

One explicit comparison between two unlike things is from this first line of a Romantic poem by William Wordsworth (1770-1850): "I wandered lonely as a cloud."

A person is NOT a cloud, but he is being likened to one in that he is floating aimlessly and solitarily across the landscape.

Some more examples of **SIMILES**:

"*Death lies on her like an untimely frost.*"

Juliet's father in Shakespeare's *Romeo and Juliet*

" *The apple-green car with the white vinyl roof and Florida plates turned into the street like a greased cobra.* **"**

Gloria Naylor's The Women of Brewster Place

" *Draw the stroke with grace, like a bird landing on the branch, not an executioner chopping off a devil's head.* **"**

Amy Tan's The Bonesetter's Daughter

223 | METAPHOR

In its more narrow sense, a figure of speech in which one thing is described in terms of another using an **IMPLICIT** *or implied comparison, without the use of "like" or "as."*

Here is a line from Alfred Noyes's poem "The Highwayman": "The moon was a ghostly galleon tossed upon cloudy seas."

The moon is NOT a galleon (a large sailing ship from the 16th to 18th centuries), but in some respects it is LIKE a ship, and the clouds are LIKE waves. The omission of "like" or "as" makes the comparison strong and direct.

Some more examples of **METAPHORS**:

In the movie *The Dark Knight*, the Joker compares himself to a dog and a wrench when he tells Batman, "You know what I am? I'm a dog chasing cars. I wouldn't know what to do if I caught one. I'm a wrench in the gears."

In Shakespeare's *As You Like It*, the cynical Jacques gives his famous seven ages of man speech in which he compares the world to a stage, life to a play, and people to the actors:

" *All the world's a stage*

And all the men and women merely players:

They have their exits and their entrances;

And one man in his time plays many parts. **"**

224 | PERSONIFICATION

A figure of speech in which an inanimate object is given human qualities or abilities

PERSONIFICATION is often used in literary works to enhance the mood or power of an image. In "I Wandered Lonely as a Cloud" Wordsworth describes a "host of golden daffodils" on the hillside beside the lake, giving them human actions and emotions with which he can identify:

> **"** *The waves beside them danced; but they*
> *Outdid the sparkling waves in glee.* **"**

Advertising slogans utilize **PERSONIFICATION** as well. Goldfish crackers are "the snack that smiles back."

225 | PARALLELISM/PARALLEL STRUCTURE

*A rhetorical device or **SYNTACTICAL** (relating to sentence structure) construction which involves using matching grammatical patterns to establish the equivalent relationship or importance of two or more items. **PARALLELISM** provides balance and authority to sentences.*

Here is an illustration of a sentence where **PARALLEL STRUCTURE** is used in two places:

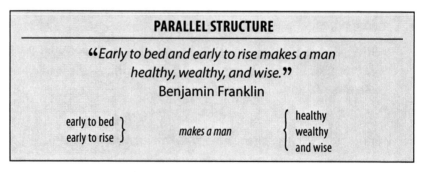

PARALLEL STRUCTURE

> **"** *Early to bed and early to rise makes a man*
> *healthy, wealthy, and wise.* **"**
> Benjamin Franklin

early to bed
early to rise } *makes a man* { healthy
wealthy
and wise

Shane was torn between achieving his goal of forgetting his past and starting a new life or saving his friends in the valley.

Note that all four ideas are expressed with the "-ing" form of the verbs.

Lies are usually told to protect the teller and to deceive the listener. Note the repetition of the "to" in the infinitive form of the **PARALLEL** ideas.

Charles Dickens's novels are full of rich **PARALLELISM**. Here is one example from the novel *Great Expectations*, with part of the young boy Pip's description of the "fearful man" he has encountered:

"A man with no hat, and with broken shoes, and with an old rag tied round his head. A man who had been soaked in water, and smothered in mud, and lamed by stones, and cut by flints, and stung by nettles, and torn by briars; who limped, and shivered, and glared and growled; and whose teeth chattered in his head as he seized me by the chin.**"**

226 | IRONY

A figure of speech in which what we say or write conveys the opposite of its literal meaning

IRONY involves the perception that things are not what they are said to be or what they seem.

Here are some examples of **IRONY**:

In *Star Wars*, Han Solo tells Jabba the Hutt, "Jabba, you're a wonderful human being." Jabba is, in fact, neither wonderful nor a human being!

In Shakespeare's *Julius Caesar*, Marc Antony gives a famous IRONIC speech in which he repeats "And Brutus is an honorable man," when Brutus has just killed Julius Caesar and is not honorable at all!

In Sophocles' *Oedipus Rex* it is **IRONIC** that Oedipus thinks he is the detective in finding out who killed his predecessor, when he is actually, **IRONICALLY**, the murderer.

227 | SYNOPSIS

A brief summary of the major points of a thesis, theory, story or literary work; an abstract; a PRÉCIS

Has anyone ever asked you to summarize a movie, television show, or a YouTube clip? If you did, you provided them with a **SYNOPSIS** or brief summary. Here is a **SYNOPSIS** of the movie *The Hangover:* Three groomsmen inexplicably lose their soon-to-be-married buddy during a wild bachelor party in Las Vegas and must try to find him by following strange clues that include a tiger, a missing tooth, and a six-month-old baby. The sequel, *The Hangover Part II*, has a similar **SYNOPSIS**. The four men wake up after a wild night in Bangkok and must piece together what happened to them while they also search for a missing member of the wedding party.

228 | SATIRE, LAMPOON, PARODY

A work that ridicules human vices and follies; comic criticism. Note that LAMPOON and PARODY are often used as verbs meaning to ridicule.

The ancient Greek playwright Aristophanes mastered the art of using **SATIRE** to mock public figures. In his play *The Clouds*, Aristophanes **LAMPOONS** Socrates as an **ABSTRUSE** (very abstract, hard to understand) philosopher who operates a "Thinking Shop." Perched in a basket suspended from the ceiling, Socrates teaches his students how to prove anything, even if it is false.

Many centuries later, *Saturday Night Live* is still using **SATIRE** to mock public figures and popular culture. *SNL* skits frequently are **PARODIES** of political speeches and debates, meant to **SATIRIZE** political figures. The *SNL* cast members are famous for their **PARODIES** of celebrities. Tina Fey **SATIRIZED** Sarah Palin, Andy Samberg often **LAMPOONS** Facebook founder Mark Zuckerberg, and Will Ferrell played Alex Trebek in *SNL's Celebrity Jeopardy* **PARODIES**.

229 | HYPERBOLE

A figure of speech in which exaggeration is used for emphasis or effect; extreme exaggeration

Have you ever exaggerated something to make a point? We all do, often for comic effect. In show business these exaggerations are called hype. In literature and daily life they are called **HYPERBOLES**. Here is a list of some commonly used **HYPERBOLES**:

"I'm so tired I could sleep for a year."

"I'm so hungry I could eat a horse."

"This book weighs a ton."

230 | CARICATURE

A representation in which the subject's distinctive features or peculiarities are deliberately exaggerated for comic effect

Do you look at the editorial cartoons in your local newspaper? Editorial cartoonists often incorporate **CARICATURES** of political figures into their cartoons. For example, Thomas Nast's **CARICATURES** of Boss Tweed helped to focus public attention on the Tweed Ring's corrupt practices. Modern cartoonists often **CARICATURE** Jay Leno by exaggerating his already-prominent chin.

231 | EPIC

A long narrative poem written in a grand style to celebrate the feats of a legendary hero

SAGA

A long narrative story; a heroic tale

Both **EPICS** and **SAGAS** are long and feature the feats of heroes. The two literary forms differ in that an **EPIC** is a narrative poem and a **SAGA** is a narrative story written in prose.

Homer's *Iliad* is the first and arguable the best **EPIC** in Western literature. Other famous **EPICS** include Virgil's *Aeneid*, Homer's *The Odyssey*, and Milton's *Paradise Lost*. J.K. Rowling's series of seven Harry Potter novels provide a contemporary example of a literary **SAGA**, while George Lucas' six Star Wars films provide a contemporary example of a cinematic **SAGA**.

Note: **EPIC** as an adjective means grand, sweeping, of historical or legendary importance.

232 | FORESHADOWING

A suggestion or indication that something will happen in a story; a hint that PRESAGES (Word 323)

The conclusion of *Batman Begins* **FORESHADOWS** the Caped Crusader's coming battle with the Joker. As the film ends, Lieutenant Gordon unveils a Bat-Signal for Batman. He then mentions a criminal who, like Batman, has "a taste for the theatrical," leaving a Joker card at his crime scenes. Batman promises to investigate, thus **FORESHADOWING** his coming confrontation with the Joker in *The Dark Knight*.

233 | ANECDOTE

A short account of an interesting or humorous incident

World-renowned physicist Albert Einstein and Anthony Kiedis, the lead singer of the Red Hot Chili Peppers, were both very good at telling interesting **ANECDOTES**.

Albert Einstein was often asked to explain the general theory of relativity. "Put your hand on a hot stove for a minute, and it seems like an hour," he once declared. "Sit with a pretty girl for an hour, and it seems like a minute. That's relativity."

An **ANECDOTE** Anthony Kiedis told about being the opening act for the Rolling Stones:

"Opening for the Stones is a crummy job...First you get there and they won't let you do a sound check. Then they give you an eightieth of the stage. They set aside this tiny area and say, 'This is for you. You don't get the lights, and you're not allowed to use our sound system. And oh, by the way, you see that wooden floor? That's Mick's imported antique wood flooring from the Brazilian jungle, and that's what he dances on. If you so much as look at it, you won't get paid.'**"**

Note: **ANECDOTAL**, the adjective form of **ANECDOTE**, has become a somewhat negative word applied to an attempt to support an opinion with only an isolated or personal example based on casual or informal observations. Others would reject **ANECDOTAL** evidence as too slim and unscientific to be persuasive.

234 | EULOGY

*A **LAUDATORY** (Word 91) speech or written tribute, especially one praising someone who has died*

EULOGY comes from the Greek prefix EU-, meaning "good" and the root LOGOS, meaning "word."

EULOGY is often **CONFLATED** (brought together, fused) with **ELEGY**, which is a poem of lament and praise for the dead. You would not speak ill (publicly) of the dead, so an **ELEGY** could also be a **EULOGY**! **ELEGY** yields the tone words **ELEGIAC** or **ELEGIACAL**, which mean sad, mournful, and **PLAINTIVE**.

Here are some noteworthy **EULOGIES**:

Mark Antony's fictional **EULOGY** for Julius Caesar in Shakespeare's play *Julius Caesar*

Ossie Davis's **EULOGY** for Malcolm X

Earl Spencer's **EULOGY** for his sister Diana, Princess of Wales

On the lighter side, in the movie *Zoolander*, Derek *Zoolander* delivered a **EULOGY** for his friends who died in the "Orange Mocha Frappuccino" gas fight.

KNOW YOUR ROOTS		
GREEK PREFIX:	EULOGY	a speech of praise
EU | good	EUPHEMISM	an inoffensive word substituted for an offensive one
	EUPHONY	a pleasing sound
	EUGENICS	the science of improving offspring
	EUPHORIA	a feeling of well-being, an almost excessive feeling of buoyant vigor and health
	EUTHANASIA	a method of causing a painless, peaceful death

235 | ALLUSION

An indirect or brief reference to a person, event, place, phrase, piece of art, or literary work that assumes a common knowledge with the reader or listener

Many contemporary songs and TV shows contain clever **ALLUSIONS** to works of literature. For example, in her song "Love Story," Taylor Swift makes **ALLUSIONS** to Shakespeare's play *Romeo and Juliet* and Hawthorne's novel *Scarlet Letter* when she warns her romantic lover, "Cause you were Romeo, I was a scarlet letter." The TV show *Gossip Girl* often uses literary **ALLUSIONS** in the titles of its episodes. For example, the episode "The Serena Also Rises" is an **ALLUSION** to Hemingway's novel *The Sun Also Rises*.

CHAPTER 8

Science And
The Social Sciences | *236 – 280*

Many students believe that SAT words are obscure and rarely used by anyone except test writers at the Educational Testing Service. Nothing could be further from the truth. Newspapers, magazines, and Internet blogs frequently use SAT vocabulary words. Front page headlines describe "**WATERSHED** events," financial articles discuss "**LUCRATIVE** deals," and editorials urge politicians to "reach a **CONSENSUS**" on important issues.

This chapter highlights 45 key words taken from science and the social sciences. While all have appeared on the SAT, they are also everyday words that you encounter in school and on the internet. Since memorizing lists is inefficient and ineffective, we have provided vivid examples designed to help you make a permanent connection with each word.

A SCIENCE: THE SAT TAKES YOU TO THE SCIENCE LAB AND BEYOND

236 | CATALYST

*In chemistry, a **CATALYST** is a substance (such as an enzyme) that accelerates the rate of a chemical reaction at some temperature, but without itself being transformed or consumed by the reaction. In everyday usage a **CATALYST** is any agent that provokes or triggers change.*

Both Rosa Parks and Rachel Carson were **CATALYSTS** whose actions helped provoke historic changes. Rosa Parks's refusal to give up her bus seat acted as a **CATALYST** that helped spark the Montgomery Bus Boycott. Today, Rosa Parks is hailed as one of the pioneers of the modern civil rights movement. Rachel Carson's book *Silent Spring* was a **CATALYST** that triggered a national campaign to limit the indiscriminate use of DDT and other harmful pesticides. Today, Rachel Carson is hailed as one of the pioneers of the modern environmental movement.

237 | CAUSTIC

*In chemistry, a **CAUSTIC** substance is one that burns or destroys organic tissue by chemical action. Hydrofluoric acid and silver nitrate are examples of **CAUSTIC** substances. In everyday usage, a **CAUSTIC** comment is one that hurts or burns.*

In the movie *Ever After*, Danielle asked her wicked stepmother, "Was there ever a time, even in its smallest measure, when you loved me?" The insensitive stepmother replied, "How can anyone love a pebble in their shoe?" Ouch! Now that was a **CAUSTIC** remark!

As a judge on *American Idol*, Simon Cowell was famous for the **CAUSTIC** barbs he directed at **INEPT** (Word 114) contestants. He told one would-be singer, "If your lifeguard duties were as good as your singing, a lot of people would be drowning." Ouch! Now that was a **CAUSTIC** remark!

238 | CRYSTALLIZE

In chemistry, CRYSTALLIZATION is the process by which crystals are formed. In everyday usage, to CRYSTALLIZE means to give a definite form to an idea or plan.

In both the classic TV show and the recent movie, the A-Team was a fictional group of soldiers of fortune led by John "Hannibal" Smith. Hannibal was especially pleased when one of his elaborate ideas **CRYSTALLIZED** into a successful plan. Like the **WILY** (clever) Hannibal, you must be **METICULOUS** (Word 8) as you design a plan to ace the SAT. In addition to studying *Direct Hits*, you might also check out "Silverturtle's Guide to SAT and Admissions Success" at CollegeConfidential.com. Silverturtle does a great job of **CRYSTAL-LIZING** valuable information.

239 | OSMOSIS

In chemistry, OSMOSIS refers to the diffusion of a fluid through a semi-permeable membrane until there is an equal concentration of fluid on both sides of the membrane. In everyday usage, OSMOSIS refers to a gradual, often unconscious process of assimilation.

What do students studying for the SAT and the Holy Roman Emperor Charlemagne have in common? Charlemagne valued education and tried so hard to study Latin that he had tablets with vocabulary words placed under his pillow. Charlemagne apparently hoped he could learn difficult words by **OSMOSIS**. Like Charlemagne, modern SAT students have to learn difficult new words. But don't put this book under your pillow. **OSMOSIS** didn't work for Charlemagne, and it won't work for you! The words in this book can only be learned by studying and using them.

240 | SEDENTARY

In ecology, animals that are SEDENTARY remain or live in one area. In everyday usage, SEDENTARY means settled and therefore accustomed to sitting or doing little exercise.

What do fungus beetles and the humans in the movie *WALL-E* have in common? Both live **SEDENTARY** lives. Fungus beetles are **SEDENTARY** creatures that seldom move more than a few yards between fungi, their primary food. The humans in *WALL-E* are 28th century couch potatoes who spend most of their time reclining in chairs while staring at computer screens. As a result of this **SEDENTARY** lifestyle, the humans are **CORPULENT** (overweight, obese) and have almost lost the ability to walk.

241 | VIRULENT

In medical science, VIRULENT refers to a disease or toxin that is extremely infectious, malignant, or poisonous. In everyday usage, VIRULENT refers to language that is bitterly hostile, hateful, and antagonistic.

What do the blue-ringed octopus and the hook-nosed sea snake have in common? Both are **DIMINUTIVE** (Word 51) animals whose venom is extremely **VIRULENT**. Although only the size of a golf ball, the blue-ringed octopus can kill an adult human in minutes with its **VIRULENT** venom. Armed with venom four to eight times more **VIRULENT** than that of a cobra, the hook-nosed sea snake can easily kill almost any animal that encroaches on its territory.

On February 9, 1950, Senator Joseph McCarthy gave a **VIRULENT** speech to an audience in Wheeling, West Virginia, declaring, "I have in my hand a list of 205—a list of names known to the Secretary of State as being members of the Communist Party and who nevertheless are still working and shaping policy in the State Department."

242 | EMPIRICAL

*In science, **EMPIRICAL** means originating in or based on direct observation and experience. **EMPIRICAL** data can then be used to support or reject a hypothesis. In everyday language, **EMPIRICAL** means to be guided by practical experience, not theory.*

The process of applying to colleges can be a **DAUNTING** (intimidating) challenge. You should begin your search with a series of questions: Would you prefer to go to an urban college or one in a more **BUCOLIC** (Word 79) setting? Would you be more comfortable in a large state university or a small private college? These questions are only a first step. It is very important to be **EMPIRICAL**, to gather facts. Don't speculate about what a college is like or what test scores you will need. Be an **EMPIRICIST** and visit a number of colleges. On your visit, gather **EMPIRICAL** information by visiting dorms, observing classes, talking with students, and asking questions.

243 | ENTOMOLOGY

The scientific study of insects

Tip for a Direct Hit

Many students confuse ENTOMOLOGY with ETYMOLOGY. ENTOMOLOGY is the study of insects, while ETYMOLOGY is a branch of linguistics concerned with the history and derivation of words.

How are honeybees, strawberry ice cream, **ENTO-MOLOGISTS**, and the SAT connected? Honeybees are responsible for pollinating one-third of all the foods we eat, including strawberries, blueberries, apples, almonds, and melons. Without honeybees, all-natural strawberry ice cream would be impossible to make. The last several winters have witnessed the sudden disappearance of more than 25 percent of the Western honeybee population. **ENTOMOLOGISTS** are **MYSTIFIED** (baffled) by what is officially called colony collapse disorder.

244 | GESTATE

In science, GESTATE means to carry within the uterus from conception to delivery. In everyday language, GESTATE means to conceive and develop in the mind.

Periods of **GESTATION** vary from animal to animal. For example, the period of **GESTATION** for domesticated cats and dogs is two months. In contrast, the period of **GESTATION** for elephants is almost 22 months!

Ideas, like a fetus, often require time to **GESTATE**. For example, the ideas contained in the Declaration of Independence did not suddenly spring from Jefferson's mind onto a piece of parchment. He later acknowledged that his eloquent statements about natural rights were derived from the English philosopher John Locke and had been **GESTATING** in his mind for some time.

245 | PARADIGM

In science, a PARADIGM is a framework or model of thought

In 1610, the Italian astronomer and physicist Galileo Galilei did something no other human being had ever done before. He pointed a telescope at Jupiter and observed the orbits of four of its moons. Galileo realized the force (which we now call gravity) that kept the moons of Jupiter in their orbits was the same force keeping the Earth and the other planets in their orbits around the Sun. Galileo's scientific observations **REFUTED** (proved false) the old geocentric **PARADIGM** that the Sun and all the planets revolve around the Earth. Instead, Galileo offered scientific support for Copernicus' revolutionary new heliocentric **PARADIGM** that placed the Sun in the center of the solar system. Galileo's work triggered a **MOMENTOUS** (Word 193) **PARADIGM** shift in human thought.

B   ECONOMICS: THESE WORDS ARE ABOUT DOLLARS AND SENSE

246 | ENTREPRENEUR

A person who organizes and manages a business or enterprise

Mark Zuckerberg is an American **ENTREPRENEUR** who is the co-founder of Facebook. Zuckerberg launched Facebook from his Harvard dorm room on February 4, 2004. Facebook now has over 800 million users and generates over $4 billion in revenue a year. As a result, Zuckerberg is one of the youngest billionaires in the world.

Although Zuckerberg is an **ENTREPRENEUR**, he is not an **INNOVATOR** (Word 126). Zuckerberg borrowed his original concept from a product produced by his prep school, Phillips Exeter Academy. For decades, the school published and distributed a printed manual for all its students and faculty, unofficially called the "face book." However, Zuckerberg was **PRESCIENT** (Word 390). Like other Internet pioneers, he understood the power of the Web to create an interactive community of users, and in 2010 *Vanity Fair* magazine named him #1 on its list of the Top 100 "most influential people of the Information Age."

247 | LUCRATIVE

Very profitable

Actors **COVET** (Word 32) lead roles in popular TV programs. In addition to fame, starring roles are also rewarded with **LUCRATIVE** salaries. For example, Hugh Laurie, the star of *House M.D.*, and Ashton Kutcher, who replaced Charlie Sheen on *Two And A Half Men*, earn $700,000 per episode. While established stars command the most **LUCRATIVE** salaries, newcomers can also collect big paychecks. For example, Matthew Morrison (*Glee*) and Nicole "Snooki" Polizzi (*Jersey Shore*) both earned $30,000 per episode in their first season.

248 | EXTRAVAGANT
Excessive and therefore lacking restraint

The Bugatti Veyron EB 16.4 is the world's most powerful and **EXTRA-VAGANT** car. The Veyron's 1001 horsepower engine can accelerate from 0 to 62 mph in just 2.46 seconds. The Super Sport version is the fastest street-legal production car in the world. Of course, the Veyron also consumes an **EXTRAVAGANT** amount of fuel, getting just under 6 mpg in city driving. At full throttle, the Veyron would empty its 26-gallon fuel tank in just 12 minutes. How much does this **EXTRAVAGANT** car cost? It can be yours for $2,250,880!

249 | AVARICE, CUPIDITY
Excessive desire for wealth; greed; COVETOUSNESS (Word 32)

Philosophers and religious leaders have long condemned **AVARICE**. The Greek philosopher Aristotle demonstrated his deep understanding of human nature when he wrote, "The **AVARICE** of mankind is insatiable." During the Middle Ages, Christian theologians identified **AVARICE** as one of the seven deadly sins.

The movie *The Third Man* takes place in Austria's capital city, Vienna. The city and its citizens are struggling to recover from the devastating effects of World War II. Consumed by **CUPIDITY**, Harry Lime steals penicillin from military hospitals and then sells diluted doses for **EXORBITANT** (Word 162) prices. The **ADULTERATED** (debased) antibiotic kills or cripples many of the children who use it. The film's hero, a pulp fiction writer named Joseph Cotten, confronts Lime as they ride on Vienna's famous Ferris wheel. From the top of the Ferris wheel, the people below look like tiny dots. Lime looks down and **CALLOUSLY** (Word 72) says, "Tell me, would you really feel any pity if one of these dots stopped moving forever? If I offered you $20,000 for every dot that you stopped, would you really tell me to keep my money, or would you calculate how many dots you could afford to spare?" Appalled by Lime's **CUPIDITY**, Cotten agrees to help police capture his villainous former friend.

250 | GLUT, PLETHORA, SURFEIT
A surplus or excess of something

While our used-car lots now have a **GLUT** of gas-guzzling vehicles, our landfills are filling up with a **PLETHORA** of old computers, printers, TVs, and other unwanted consumer electronic goods. Americans are now throwing away two million tons of electronic trash, or e-waste, each year. While there is a **SURFEIT** of outdated e-waste, there is currently a **PAUCITY** (Word 4) of recycling options. The Environmental Protection Agency estimates that we recycle only 350,000 tons of e-waste each year.

251 | DESTITUTE, IMPOVERISHED, INDIGENT
Very poor, lacking basic resources
AFFLUENT, OPULENT
Very rich, having abundant resources

In the movie *Trading Places*, Eddie Murphy's character was originally **DESTITUTE** but became very **AFFLUENT**. In the movie *Coming to America*, Murphy played an African prince who pretended to be **IMPOVERISHED** but had in fact grown up in an **OPULENT** palace.

Eddie Murphy's characters were both fictional. In the movie *The Pursuit of Happyness*, Will Smith portrayed the real life story of how Chris Gardner lost all of his family's savings by investing in a franchise selling bone density scanners. As a result, Chris became **INDIGENT**, and he and his young son were forced to spend nights riding buses and sleeping in subway restrooms. Chris ultimately became **AFFLUENT** by learning how to become a successful stock broker.

252 | MUNIFICENT
Very generous

What do Oprah Winfrey, Angelina Jolie, and Brad Pitt have in common? All three are celebrities known for their **MUNIFICENT** donations to charities. Oprah is regularly the world's most **MUNIFICENT** celebrity donor. Her annual donations of $40-50 million have made her the greatest black philanthropist in American history. Angelina Jolie and Brad Pitt also showed their **MUNIFICENCE** when they gave $8.4 million to their Jolie-Pitt Foundation. Their **LARGESSE** (generosity) is enabling the Make It Right Project to build 150 green houses in New Orleans's Lower 9th Ward, which was devastated by Hurrican Katrina.

253 | PARSIMONIOUS

Excessively cheap with money; stingy

Would you want people to call you a "Scrooge"? Probably not. Ebenezer Scrooge is the leading character in *A Christmas Carol* by Charles Dickens. Scrooge lived up to his name by being very **PARSIMONIOUS**. A **PARSIMONIOUS** person would be the **ANTITHESIS** (Word 33) of someone who is **MUNIFICENT** (Word 252).

254 | DEPRECIATION

Any decrease or loss in value caused by age, wear, or market conditions

DEPRECIATION means that values are going down! The stock market Crash of 1929 caused a severe **DEPRECIATION** in the value of stocks. By 1932, stocks listed on the New York Stock Exchange were worth just 11 percent of their pre-Crash value. **DEPRECIATION** is not limited to historic examples found only in textbooks. In the last two years, American homeowners collectively lost more than $2 trillion in home value as their properties **DEPRECIATED**.

255 | REMUNERATE

To compensate; to make payment for; to pay a person

REMUNERATION varies greatly from job to job. On July 24, 2009, the Federal minimum wage rose from $6.55 per hour to $7.25 per hour.

The President of the United States earns $400,000 per year, and the Vice-President earns $227,300. In contrast, in 2011 Tiger Woods was still the top paid athlete in the world, having earned approximately $75 million.

C. HISTORY AND GEOGRAPHY: THESE WORDS WILL HELP YOU UNDERSTAND PEOPLE, PLACES, AND EVENTS

256 | ACCORD

A formal concurrence, agreement, or harmony of minds

In *Pirates of the Caribbean: The Curse of the Black Pearl*, Captain Jack Sparrow and Will reach an **ACCORD**. Will agrees to free Sparrow, and then Sparrow agrees to help Will find Elizabeth. In world affairs, nations also sign **ACCORDS**. For example, the Helsinki **ACCORDS** (1975) recognized basic human rights, and the Camp David **ACCORDS** (1978) provided a framework for establishing peaceful relations between Egypt and Israel.

257 | ENLIGHTEN, EDIFY

To inform, instruct, illuminate, and thus remove darkness and ignorance

During the Enlightenment, writers such as Voltaire **ENLIGHTENED** European society by urging people to use science and reason instead of blindly following inherited prejudices. Voltaire took it upon himself to **EDIFY** France single-handedly. He wrote about 70 volumes of various kinds of literature.

In cartoons and comics, a light-bulb appears over someone's head when the person suddenly understands something because he or she is **ENLIGHTENED**!

258 | APPEASEMENT

The policy of granting concessions to maintain peace

Would you **APPEASE** a crying child by giving him or her a piece of candy? Would you **APPEASE** a bully who threatened to beat you up? Are there times when **APPEASEMENT** is a wise policy? The British Prime Minister Neville Chamberlain thought so. At the Munich Conference in September 1938, Chamberlain **APPEASED** Hitler by agreeing to his demand to control the Sudetenland. When he returned to London, Chamberlain told cheering crowds, "I believe it is peace for our time." Chamberlain's prediction proved to be tragically wrong.

259 | NULLIFY

To make null; declare invalid

The tariffs of 1828 and 1832 infuriated John C. Calhoun of South Carolina. Led by Calhoun, South Carolina voted to **NULLIFY** or invalidate the tariffs. President Jackson rejected **NULLIFICATION** by saying that it was treason and that those implementing it were traitors. The crisis was averted when Henry Clay devised a compromise in which the tariffs were gradually lowered.

260 | TRIUMVIRATE

A group or association of three leaders

John C. Calhoun, Henry Clay, and Daniel Webster were a group of three American statesmen known as "The Great Triumvirate," who dominated the U.S. Senate during the 1830s and 1840s. While the term **TRIUMVIRATE** usually refers to political leaders, it can be used to describe any group of three (the prefix *tri* means three). For example, the videogame console market is dominated by the **TRIUMVIRATE** of Nintendo's Wii, Sony's PS3, and Microsoft's Xbox 360.

261 | PRETEXT

An excuse; an alleged cause

On August 2 and 4, 1964, two American destroyers patrolling international waters in the Gulf of Tonkin reported that they had been fired upon by North Vietnamese PT boats. While later investigations strongly suggested that the North Vietnamese fired in self-defense on August 2 and the "attack" of August 4 never happened, President Johnson used the alleged attacks as a **PRETEXT** to ask Congress for broader powers. The **PRETEXT** worked. Congress promptly passed the *Tonkin Gulf Resolution*, giving Johnson a blank check to escalate the war in Southeast Asia.

262 | WATERSHED

Critical point that marks a change of course; a turning point

This generation of Americans has experienced a **WATERSHED** event that riveted the entire nation and marked a crucial historic turning point. On January 20, 2009, a record crowd of approximately 1.5 million people watched Chief Justice John Roberts swear-in Barack Obama as the 44th President of the United States. The inauguration marked an historic **WATERSHED** in American history as Obama became America's first African-American president. For millions of people in the United States and around the world, the inauguration marked the fulfillment of Dr. King's dream and the beginning of a new era in American political history.

263 | CONSENSUS

A general agreement

Do you think there is a need to develop and use more alternative energy sources? If you answer yes to this question, you are part of a growing national **CONSENSUS** on this issue. Soaring gasoline prices have forced Americans to realize that we cannot indefinitely continue to import 70 percent of our oil at an annual cost of $700 billion. Note that a **CONSENSUS** does not mean that everyone must be in complete agreement with a policy or a decision. While there is a **CONSENSUS** that America must develop new sources of energy, there is not yet a **CONSENSUS** on which of the **MYRIAD** (Word 345) proposed alternative energy solutions should be utilized.

264 | AUTOCRAT, DESPOT

A ruler or other person with unlimited power and authority

In the movie *300*, Xerxes is portrayed as an **AUTOCRAT** who is determined to conquer and enslave the freedom-loving Greeks. However, led by Sparta and Athens, the Greeks successfully defeat Xerxes, thus defending democracy. Although democracy continues to make great strides, the modern world still has countries ruled by **AUTOCRATS**. For example, Kim Jong-il wields absolute power over North Korea. Known to his people as "Dear Leader," the **AUTOCRATIC** Kim brutally suppresses dissidents and maintains the world's fourth largest army. While his **IMPOVERISHED** (Word 251) people suffer from repeated famines, their **DESPOTIC** "Dear Leader" dines on steak and sips expensive imported wines.

265 | MANIFESTO

A public declaration of beliefs, policies, or intentions

MANIFESTOS are not written by people who are self-satisfied and complacent. They are written by people who are **INDIGNANT** (Word 65) and demand a change. For example, in 1848 a small but determined group of feminists held a Women's Rights Convention at Seneca Falls, New York. Led by the defiant Elizabeth Cady Stanton, they issued a **MANIFESTO** called the "Declaration of Sentiments," which boldly declared that "all men and women are created equal." The **MANIFESTO** launched the modern women's rights movement.

266 | ENFRANCHISE

To endow with the rights of citizenship, especially the right to vote

DISENFRANCHISE

To deprive of some privilege or right, especially the right to vote

In American history, Jim Crow laws **DISENFRANCHISED** African-American voters, while the Voting Rights Act of 1965 **ENFRANCHISED** African-American voters. Ratified in 1920, the 19th Amendment **ENFRANCHISED** millions of American women. The 26th Amendment **ENFRANCHISED** 18-year-old American citizens.

267 | COERCE

To force to act or think in a certain way by use of pressure, threats, or torture; to compel

Joseph Stalin ruled the Soviet Union as an **AUTOCRAT** (Word 264) from 1924 until his death in 1953. Stalin used terror to **COERCE** the Russian people to unquestioningly follow his leadership. In the *Gulag Archipelago*, Alexander Solzhenitsyn describes a Communist Party conference in which officials respond to a call for a tribute to Comrade Stalin with "stormy applause." The ovation continued because secret police "were standing in the hall applauding and waiting to see who would quit first!" The threat of **COERCION** worked: "The applause went on—six, seven, eight minutes!" Finally after 11 minutes the director of a paper factory stopped applauding and sat down. Solzhenitsyn explains, "That was how they discovered who the independent people were." In a frightening demonstration of **COERCION**, the authorities arrested the factory director and sentenced him to ten years in a labor camp. In a chilling reminder of the power of a totalitarian state to **COERCE** conformity, the interrogator reminded the former factory director, "Don't ever be the first to stop applauding."

268 | EGALITARIAN

Favoring social equality; believing in a society in which all people have equal political, economic, and civil rights

During the 19th century, American utopian leaders were inspired by a dream of creating **EGALITARIAN** communities. Founded in 1848 by John Humphrey Noyes, the Oneida Community in upstate New York became a flourishing **EGALITARIAN** commune of some 300 people. Men and women shared equally in all the community's tasks, from field to factory to kitchen. The members lived in one building and ate in a common dining hall. The dream of **EGALITARIAN** living did not last. The communal dining hall ultimately became a restaurant. Led by Noyes's son, Pierrepont, Oneida Community, Ltd. grew into the world's leading manufacturer of stainless steel knives, forks, and spoons, with annual sales of a half billion dollars.

269 | DEMARCATION

The setting or marking of boundaries or limits, as a line of demarcation

What is the relationship between the SAT word **DEMARCATION** and the reason why Brazil is the only Portuguese-speaking country in the Americas? Columbus' **WATERSHED** (Word 262) voyage created an **ACRIMONIOUS** (Word 196) dispute between Spain and Portugal over the rights to lands in the New World. The two nations avoided an **IMPASSE** (Word 28) by agreeing to the 1494 Treaty of Tordesillas. Under the terms of this agreement, Spain and Portugal divided the non-Christian world into two zones of influence. The line of **DEMARCATION** gave Portugal a claim to Brazil.

270 | INQUISITION

A severe interrogation; a systematic questioning

The **INQUISITION** was a formal court of justice established (1232-1820) by the Roman Catholic Church to discover and suppress **HERESY** (false beliefs). Although the United States has never had a formal court of **INQUISITION**, numerous zealots have conducted **INQUISITIONS** into the conduct of public officials. The best known of these **INQUISITIONS** was conducted by Senator Joseph McCarthy during the early 1950s. McCarthy ruthlessly questioned public officials as part of his campaign against alleged Communists. Instigated by McCarthyism, Hollywood "blacklists" unfairly **STIGMATIZED** (branded) screen writers, actors, and directors as Communist sympathizers.

271 | AMELIORATE

To make a situation better

EXACERBATE

To make a situation worse

What do Dorothea Dix, Ida B. Wells-Barnett, and Batman have in common? All three were crusaders who dedicated themselves to **AMELIORATING** social problems. Dorothea Dix worked to **AMELIORATE** the lives of the **INDIGENT** (Word 251) insane by creating the first generation of American mental hospitals. Ida B. Wells-Barnett worked to **AMELIORATE** the lives of African-Americans by exposing the problem of lynching in the South. And Batman worked to **AMELIORATE** the lives of the citizens of Gotham City by fighting the power of its crime bosses. Interestingly, Batman learned that **PARADOXICALLY** (Word 41), his efforts also **EXACERBATED** Gotham's crime problem by leading to an escalation of violence.

272 | DESICCATED

Thoroughly dried out; lifeless, totally arid

Antarctica is technically a desert that receives less than two inches of precipitation a year. One interior region of the Antarctic is known as the Dry Valleys. These valleys have not seen rainfall in over two million years. The Dry Valleys exist because 100 mph Katabatic downwinds **DESICCATE** all moisture. The freezing temperatures and the absence of water and all life simulate conditions on the

Planet Mars. As a result, the region is used as a training ground for astronauts who may one day make a voyage to the equally-**DESICCATED** Red Planet.

273 | CONTIGUOUS

Sharing an edge or boundary; touching

Tip for a Direct Hit

CONTIGUOUS means that two objects actually touch. In contrast, PROXIMITY means that two objects are very near in space or time. On a city street, two CONTIGUOUS businesses touch each other, while two businesses separated by other stores share a close PROXIMITY to each other.

Which of the following is the southernmost city in the 48 **CONTIGUOUS** states?

A) Kaalualu, Hawaii

B) Key West, Florida

The answer depends upon the meaning of the word **CONTIGUOUS**. Since the 48 **CONTIGUOUS** or touching states do not include Hawaii (or Alaska), the correct answer is B. Hawaii is actually an **ARCHIPELAGO** (chain of islands) located in the central Pacific Ocean about 2,000 miles southwest of the 48 **CONTIGUOUS** states.

D LAW AND ORDER: THESE WORDS WILL HELP YOU UNDERSTAND HOW THE WHEELS OF JUSTICE TURN

274 | PERTINENT

Relevant; to the point; clearly illustrative of a major point

In the movie *Remember the Titans*, team captain Gerry criticizes fellow player Julius for selfish play and not listening to the coaches. Julius defends himself by asking Gerry these **PERTINENT** questions: "Why should I give a hoot about you or anybody else out there? You are the Captain, right? Then why don't you tell your white buddies to block for Rev or Plugged Nickel? I'm supposed to wear myself out for the team. What team?" Gerry reacts by saying "That's the worst attitude I ever heard," but Julius responds with a **PERTINENT** point: "Attitude reflects leadership, Captain."

275 | COMPLICITY

Association or participation in a wrongful act

Tupac Shakur (2Pac) is widely believed to be one of America's greatest and most successful rappers, with 75 million albums sold worldwide and over 50 million in the United States. On September 7, 1996, Shakur was shot four times in a drive-by shooting in Las Vegas. He died six days later. Because of their bitter rivalry with 2Pac, rappers Biggie Smalls and Sean Combs were suspected of being **COMPLICIT** in the murder. However, both Biggie and Combs vigorously denied any **COMPLICITY** in 2Pac's death. Despite many investigations, the case remains unsolved.

276 | EXONERATE, EXCULPATE

To free from guilt or blame

What do Benjamin Franklin Gates (*National Treasure: Book of Secrets*) and Harry Potter have in common? They both **EXONERATED** members of their families of **EXECRABLE** (Word 389) crimes. Ben successfully **EXCULPATED** his great-great-grandfather, Thomas Gates, of **COMPLICITY** (Word 275) in the plot to assassinate Abraham Lincoln. Harry successfully **EXONERATED** his godfather Sirius Black of the murder of Peter Pettigrew and 12 Muggles.

277 | INDISPUTABLE

Not open to question; undeniable; irrefutable

Who killed President Kennedy? The Warren Commission published a comprehensive report providing what it believed was **INDISPUTABLE** evidence that Lee Harvey Oswald acted alone. However, **SKEPTICS** (Word 102) soon criticized the Warren Commission's findings. In the movie *JFK*, director Oliver Stone presents what he considers **INDISPUTABLE** evidence that Lee Harvey Oswald was in fact part of a secret conspiracy to kill President Kennedy.

278 | PRECEDENT

An act or instance that is used as an example in dealing with subsequent similar instances

Suppose you were part of a group scheduled to visit the White House and meet the President. How would you address the President, and upon meeting him (or her), what would you do? These issues have been settled by long-established **PRECEDENTS**. Washington rejected "His Highness" and "His High Mightiness" for the simple greeting "Mr. President." After saying "Mr. President, it is an honor to meet you," would you bow or shake hands? Although Washington favored bowing, Thomas Jefferson thought the practice too royal. He established the **PRECEDENT** of shaking hands, feeling that this gesture was more democratic.

KNOW YOUR ROOTS		
LATIN ROOT: *CEDE, CEED, CESS* | to go	CEDE	to admit a point in an argument
	ACCEDE	to go along with, to agree to
	CONCEDE	to yield to, agree to a loss in an election
	INTERCEDE	to go between two litigants
	PRECEDE	to go before
	RECEDE	to go back
	SECEDE	to go apart, to leave a group, like the Union
	EXCEED	to go beyond the ordinary
	PROCEED	to go forth
	SUCCEED	to gain something good, like a goal
	ACCESSION	a going to, like an accession to the throne
	RECESSION	a going back, a decline in the economy

279 | UNPRECEDENTED

Without previous example, never known before

Will Smith has achieved **UNPRECEDENTED** success in his career. He began as a moderately successful rapper and then launched his acting career with the show *The Fresh Prince of Bel-Air*. Smith said that he began acting with the goal of becoming the biggest movie star in the world. A remarkable 14 of his films have grossed over $100 million worldwide. This **UNPRECEDENTED** achievement has propelled Smith to the A-list and established him as the most marketable movie star in Hollywood. His successful career will no doubt continue with the release of *Men in Black III* in 2012.

280 | MALFEASANCE

Misconduct or wrongdoing, especially by a public official

After numerous charges of **MALFEASANCE,** on January 29, 2009, the Illinois State Senate found Governor Rod Blagojevich guilty of the charges of impeachment. FBI phone wiretaps recorded Blagojevich **BLATANTLY** (unmistakably) discussing the possibility of selling the U.S. Senate seat vacated by then-President-elect Barack Obama. "The seat," the governor said, "is a valuable thing; you don't just give it away for nothing." Blagojevich's **MALFEASANCE** did not stop with soliciting bids for a vacant Senate seat. He also abused his power by withholding an $8 million appropriation for a children's hospital unless the hospital's chief executive came through with an anticipated campaign contribution.

CHAPTER 9

Words With Multiple Meanings | *281 – 302*

Learning new vocabulary words is a challenge when a word has a single meaning. Many students are surprised to discover that there are words that have multiple meanings. For example, everyone knows that a flag is a rectangular piece of fabric with a distinctive design that is used to symbolize a nation. But **FLAG** can also mean to lose energy or interest.

SAT test writers have long been aware of words with multiple meanings. Students who know only one of the meanings often eliminate the word and miss the question. In fact, words like **FLAG** and **CHECK** are among the most-missed words on the SAT.

This chapter will examine and illustrate 22 commonly-used words with multiple meanings. Our focus will be on these words' secondary definitions, the ones SAT test writers use to test your knowledge. So be prepared to learn that everyday words like **CHECK**, **COIN**, and even **PEDESTRIAN** have less commonly-used secondary meanings.

281 | ARREST

To bring to a stop; halt

What is the first thing you think of when you hear the word **ARREST**? For most, **ARREST** probably calls to mind a police officer and handcuffs. **ARREST** does mean to seize and hold under the authority of the law.

The word **ARREST** has other meanings. SAT test writers will use **ARREST** to mean to bring to a stop or halt. Environmentalists, for example, hope to **ARREST** the growth of carbon dioxide emissions in the earth's atmosphere. One way to remember this use of **ARREST** is to think of a cardiac **ARREST**. This condition takes place when there is an abrupt stoppage of normal blood circulation due to heart failure.

282 | GRAVITY

Seriousness; dignity; solemnity; weight

Everyone has heard the expression, "Whatever goes up, must come down." This saying is true because of the law of **GRAVITY**. In physics, **GRAVITY** refers to the natural force of attraction exerted by a celestial body.

On October 22, 1962, President Kennedy informed a stunned nation that the Soviet Union had **SURREPTITIOUSLY** (Word 17) placed intermediate-range nuclear missiles in Cuba. The President underscored the **GRAVITY** of the crisis when he ordered a naval blockade of Cuba and sternly warned that the United States would react to any missile launched from Cuba with a "full retaliatory response upon the Soviet Union."

283 | PRECIPITATE

To cause, bring about prematurely, hastily, or suddenly

Most people associate the word **PRECIPITATION** with rain, snow, or sleet. However, **PRECIPITATE** can also refer to a result or outcome of an action. Test writers often use **PRECIPITATE** on AP US History questions, as when the discovery of Soviet missiles in Cuba **PRECIPITATED** the Cuban Missile Crisis.

In chemistry, a **PRECIPITATE** is a substance that separates out of a solution or a result of a chemical reaction.

284 | RELIEF
Elevation of a land surface

What is the first thing that comes to your mind when you hear the word **RELIEF**? In everyday usage, **RELIEF** most commonly refers to the feeling of ease when a burden has been removed or lightened. For example, in baseball a **RELIEF** pitcher eases the burden of the starting pitcher. However, **RELIEF** can also be used as a geographic term that refers to the elevation of a land surface. For example, **RELIEF** maps of the United States rise at the Appalachian Mountains in the East and at the Rocky Mountains in the West.

285 | CHECK
To restrain; halt; hold back; contain

We are all familiar with the word **CHECK**. We earn **CHECKS**, cash **CHECKS**, and **CHECK** our work on math problems. Airline passengers **CHECK** in at the ticket counter and hotel guests **CHECK** in at the registration counter. SAT test writers know that you are familiar with these everyday uses of the word **CHECK**. But the word **CHECK** can also mean to restrain, halt, or hold back. For example, our Constitution calls for a system of **CHECKS** and balances to restrain each branch of government. During the Cold War, the U.S. policy of containment was designed to **CHECK** the expansion of Soviet power and influence. And hockey and lacrosse fans know that a **CHECK** is when one player blocks or impedes the movement of an opponent.

286 | FLAG

To become weak, feeble, or spiritless; to lose interest

A **FLAG**, in its most familiar sense, is a banner or emblem used to symbolize a country, state, or community. However, **FLAG** can also mean to become weak or to lose interest. Whenever the singer Beyoncé wins an award, she always thanks her parents for keeping her spirits up and never letting her enthusiasm **FLAG**. She says that her parents keep her motivation strong and her mind focused. Don't let your energy **FLAG**! Keep on learning your *Direct Hits* vocabulary!

287 | DISCRIMINATING

Characterized by the ability to make fine distinctions; having refined taste

Is **DISCRIMINATING** a negative or a positive word? Actually, it can be both. Most people consider **DISCRIMINATING** a negative word because it refers to the act of treating a person, racial group, or minority unfairly. Surprisingly, **DISCRIMINATING** can be a positive word when it refers to someone's ability to make fine distinctions and thus demonstrate good taste. For example, **CONNOISSEURS** (knowledgeable amateurs) are known for their **DISCRIMINATING** taste in rare wine, fine clothes, or valuable art. In the James Bond movies, Bond is a secret agent who displays **DISCRIMINATING** taste by ordering vodka martinis ("shaken, not stirred"), wearing Omega watches, and wearing stylish tuxedos.

288 | ECLIPSE

Overshadow; outshine; surpass

In astronomy, an **ECLIPSE** is the total or partial covering of one celestial body by another. A solar **ECLIPSE**, for example, occurs when the moon passes between the sun and the earth. **ECLIPSE**, however, can also be a verb, meaning to overshadow or surpass. Many hopeful singers dream of winning on *American Idol*, but the title alone does not determine their success. There have been numerous cases of other *Idol* finalists attaining major success and even **ECLIPSING** the success of the winners. Fourth-place finalist Chris Daughtry has **ECLIPSED** many *American Idol* winners in record sales, awards, and popularity. Seventh-place finisher Jennifer Hudson has **ECLIPSED** the success of many other *Idol* alumni through her album sales and awards; she even earned an Academy Award for her performance in *Dreamgirls*.

289 | COIN
To devise a new word or phrase

If you see the word **COIN** in a PSAT or SAT question, the first image that will probably come to mind will be the image of a penny, nickel, dime, or quarter. While **COIN** is most commonly used to refer to a small piece of money, it can also mean to create a new word or phrase. The English language is not static. New words are **COINED** or created all the time. For example, Janine Benyus is a natural sciences writer who **COINED** the word "biomimicry" to describe the art of copying nature's biological principles of design. Ms. Benyus **COINED** the term by combining the Greek "bios," meaning "life," and "mimesis," meaning "imitate." Architects in London are using biomimetic principles derived from ocean sponges to design more energy-efficient buildings.

290 | STOCK
A stereotypical and formulaic character in a novel or film

The word **STOCK** has 13 different definitions, ranging from the merchandise in a store to a unit of ownership in a company. While SAT test writers are aware of these different definitions, they are most interested in **STOCK** as a literary term referring to formulaic characters. Teen movies such as *Clueless, Mean Girls*, and *Superbad* all feature **STOCK** characters such as "The Perfect Girl," "The Blonde Bimbo," "The Popular Jock," and "The Awkward BUT Ultimately Beautiful Girl." These **STOCK** characters are easily recognizable but one-dimensional and **TRITE** (Word 36).

291 | CURRENCY

General acceptance or use; prevalence

What is the first thought that comes to your mind when you hear the word **CURRENCY**? Most people probably immediately think of money. However, **CURRENCY** can also refer to an idea that is becoming widespread or prevalent. For example, in his book *Quiet Strength*, Tony Dungy argues that a coach should treat his or her players with respect and avoid screaming at them. When he was Head Coach of the Indianapolis Colts, Dungy practiced what he preached. Although Dungy's view is gaining **CURRENCY**, many coaches still rely on old-fashioned **TIRADES** (Word 100) to motivate their players.

292 | BENT

A strong tendency; a leaning; an inclination; a PROPENSITY

Have you ever said, "This nail is **BENT**; I can't use it?" For most people, the word **BENT** means twisted. However, **BENT** can also mean a strong tendency or disposition to follow a particular course of action. For example, the world-famous artist Pablo Picasso demonstrated a **BENT** toward art from an early age. According to his family, Picasso's **PROPENSITY** was so great that he drew before he could talk!

In the film *Bad Teacher*, Elizabeth Halsey's **AVARICIOUS** (Word 249) **BENT** caused her to act in an immoral way. To gain money, Miss Halsey became moderator of a seventh grade charity car wash and secretly **EMBEZZLED** (stole) the profits. Worst of all, Miss Halsey's **MALEVOLENT** (Word 213) **BENT** motivated her to steal the answer key to the state standardized test in order to receive a bonus from her high school for being the teacher with the highest test scores.

293 | COURT

To attempt to gain the favor or support of a person or group; to woo

Most people associate the word **COURT** with a place. A **COURT** is where people play tennis or basketball. A **COURT** is also a place where justice is administered by a judge or a jury. But **COURT** can also be used as a verb. For example, when politicians run for office, they **COURT** votes. During the early 1970s, Richard Nixon **COURTED** the "Silent Majority," a group of voters who supported his Vietnam War policies and opposed the counterculture. In the 1980s, Ronald Reagan **COURTED** "Reagan Democrats," blue-collar workers who traditionally supported the Democratic Party. Today, candidates from both parties are working hard to **COURT** young voters.

294 | NEGOTIATE
To successfully travel through, around, or over an obstacle or terrain

The word **NEGOTIATE** is very familiar to students studying American history. Our national history is filled with examples of diplomats **NEGOTIATING** treaties and labor leaders **NEGOTIATING** contracts. But the word **NEGOTIATE** can also mean to successfully travel through, around, or over an obstacle or difficult terrain. For example, settlers traveling along the Oregon Trail had to **NEGOTIATE** their way across broad streams and over steep mountain passes. In the *Lord of the Rings* trilogy, Frodo, Bilbo, and Samwise had to **NEGOTIATE** a series of formidable obstacles before reaching the Crack of Doom in Mordor.

295 | TEMPER
To soften; to moderate; to MITIGATE (Word 31)

TEMPER is a word with contradictory meanings. On the one hand, **TEMPER** refers to a sudden burst of anger. On the other hand, to **TEMPER** means to soften or moderate one's emotions. In the movie *Happy Gilmore*, Happy illustrates both meanings of **TEMPER**. Happy loses his **TEMPER** on the golf course as he fights with Bob Barker and almost comes to blows with Shooter McGavin. Virginia successfully persuades Happy that he must **TEMPER** his anger. As a result, Happy defeats Shooter, wins over Virginia, and saves his grandmother's home.

296 | PEDESTRIAN

Undistinguished; ordinary; conventional

How can the word **PEDESTRIAN** have to do with both crosswalks and graduation speakers? **PEDESTRIANS**, or people who travel on foot, should use specially-designed crosswalks to cross busy highways. On the other hand, graduation speakers should avoid **PEDESTRIAN** statements such as "We are now beginning a new chapter in our lives" or "This is not the end but the beginning." Why do we call these age-old clichés **PEDESTRIAN**? Well, the word **PEDESTRIAN** can also mean ordinary and conventional. This is the meaning that you will encounter on your SAT!

KNOW YOUR ROOTS		
LATIN ROOT: **PED,** | foot **POD**	CENTIPEDE	a 100-footed insect
	EXPEDITE	to free one caught by the foot, remove obstacles, hasten, accelerate, facilitate
	EXPEDIENT	dispatching from the foot (literally), convenient, useful, fit, suitable for the purpose, advantageous
	EXPEDITION	a journey dispatched for a particular purpose
	IMPEDE	to hold the feet, hinder, obstruct, delay, FETTER
	IMPEDIMENT	something that holds the feet, a hindrance, an obstruction
	PEDAL	an appendage to be pushed with the foot, as on a piano or bicycle
	PEDICURE	a cleaning and polishing of the toenails
	PEDIGREE	a family lineage, based on the fact that a part of a genealogical chart looks like a *pie de grue*, a crane's foot
	PEDESTAL	the foot or foundation support for a column, lamp, or statue
	QUADRUPED	an animal that walks on all four legs
	TRIPOD	a three-footed stool or support, as for a camera

297 | CAVALIER

Having an arrogant attitude or a haughty disregard for others

Fans of NBA basketball teams and University of Virginia athletic teams will quickly recognize the word **CAVALIER** as the nickname of the Cleveland Cavaliers and the UVA Cavaliers. The nickname makes sense. During the Middle Ages a **CAVALIER** was a gallant or chivalrous man. Would this knowledge help you on the SAT? Unfortunately, it might mislead you. **CAVALIER** also describes an arrogant and haughty disregard for others. The **CAVALIER** statement "Let them eat cake" is commonly attributed to the French queen, Marie Antoinette. She supposedly made this **CAVALIER** remark upon hearing that the French people had no bread to eat. Her **CAVALIER** attitude inflamed popular **ANTAGONISM** (great dislike) toward her and may have contributed to her trip to the guillotine. Today, a **CAVALIER** attitude won't cost you your head, but it could cost you friends.

298 | SANCTION

An official approval or disapproval for an action

SANCTION is one of the few words in the English language that have diametrically opposite meanings. When it is used in a positive sense, **SANCTION** means official approval or permission. For example, if your school district **SANCTIONS** cell phones, then you have permission to bring them to school. But, when **SANCTION** is used in a negative sense, it means official disapproval and thus the risk of incurring penalties. If your school district **SANCTIONS** against cell phone use, you *don't* have permission to bring them to school. It is important to note that College Board rules impose strict **SANCTIONS** on students who forget to turn off cell phones during the SAT.

299 | COMPROMISE

To reduce the quality or value of something; to jeopardize or place at risk

American history is filled with famous compromises in which two sides settled their differences by making concessions. This use of the word **COMPROMISE** is so common that it is easy to forget that **COMPROMISE** can also mean to jeopardize the quality or value of something. For example, identify theft has **COMPROMISED** the personal information of millions of Americans. The quality of a product can be **COMPROMISED** by inferior materials. And finally, it is also possible for a cultural value to be **COMPROMISED**. Many **PUNDITS** (Word 117) believe that the values of hard work, patience, and diligence are being **COMPROMISED** by our culture's **PENCHANT** (Word 62) for instant gratification.

300 | CHANNEL
To direct or guide along a desired course

Why would the word **CHANNEL** appear on the SAT? Everybody knows that a **CHANNEL** has to do with radio and television stations. But **CHANNEL** can also mean to direct or guide along a desired course.

As portrayed in *The Social Network*, Sean Parker, the co-founder of Napster helped **CHANNEL** the creators of Facebook to success. In one scene, Sean Parker meets with the Mark Zuckerberg and Eduardo Saverin at a club in New York City to discuss the future of their brainchild. Parker **CHANNELS** the team's efforts by encouraging Zuckerberg and friends to maintain minimal advertising on Thefacebook, to move the headquarters to the technology hotspot of California, and finally to change the name of his social network from "Thefacebook" to simply "Facebook."

301 | QUALIFY
To modify; to limit by adding exceptions or restricting conditions

You are probably familiar with the meaning of **QUALIFY** that means to earn the right to take part in a game, an office, an occupation. A swimmer wants to **QUALIFY** for the state championships, that is, to post a time that meets the **QUALIFYING** standards. But it can also mean to modify or limit something. You could **QUALIFY** an endorsement of a candidate for a job by saying, "Despite his intelligence, hard work, and cheerful nature, he was often late to work." This kind of **QUALIFICATION** makes a good statement less positive. You can also **QUALIFY** or **MITIGATE** (Word 31) a negative statement. For example, "The students found the teacher to be egocentric, strict, and demanding, but they later acknowledged that he had prepared them well for college."

302 | PERSONIFICATION

A perfect example; embodiment; EPITOME; PARAGON

We encountered **PERSONIFICATION** (Word 224) as a figure of speech in which an inanimate object demonstrates human qualities. However, **PERSONIFICATION** also means a person or thing that represents or embodies a perfect example of some quality, thing, or idea. In Greek mythology the god Cupid was seen as the **PERSONIFICATION** of love.

In 1990 the South African activist Nelson Mandela emerged from 27 years in prison (for sabotage and other charges) to lead his party in the negotiations that led to a multi-racial democracy in South Africa. As president, he promoted policies to combat poverty and inequality and **PERSONIFIED** reconciliation rather than vengefulness. A **PARAGON** of statesmanship, he was awarded the 1993 Nobel Peace Prize. At the celebration of Mandela's 90th birthday, Celebration Coordinator George Ngwane said, "Mandela is the **EPITOME** of struggle and aspiration of humanity."

Though she died in 1996, Barbara Jordan, the first African American congresswoman from the South, is still admired and acclaimed as the **PERSONIFICATION** of a stateswoman. She was freshman member of the Judiciary Committee that considered articles of impeachment against President Richard M. Nixon. After explaining the reasoning behind her support of each of the five articles of impeachment against President Nixon, Jordan said that if her fellow committee members did not find the evidence compelling enough, "then perhaps the eighteenth-century Constitution should be abandoned to a twentieth-century paper shredder." Beth Rogers, in her book about Jordan, writes about her impact during the Watergate scandal: "Her riveting testimony in 1974, when she **JUXTAPOSED** (Word 426) the intent and words of the Constitution against the behavior of the president of the United States, earned her America's trust."

CHAPTER 10

The Toughest Words I | *303 – 365*

Do you know what **DILATORY, CAPITULATE**, and **BURGEON** mean? If so, congratulations! If not, don't be upset. These words are all answers or answer choices to Level 5 questions, the toughest ones on the SAT. Only about 20 percent of students correctly answer a Level 5 question.

PARADOXICALLY (Word 41), Level 5 questions are both the toughest and the easiest on the SAT. They are tough because the word choices deliberately include challenging words known to only a small percentage of students. They are easy because, if you know the words, the clues are often very straightforward and lead directly to the correct answer.

Chapters 10 and 11 focus on Level 5 vocabulary words. Each of these words was the answer to a very difficult question on a recent SAT. Knowing the meanings of these words will significantly raise your SAT score by helping you infuse great vocabulary into your essay, understand difficult critical reading passages, and master challenging sentence completion questions. Don't be **DILATORY** (late from procrastinating). There is no reason to **CAPITULATE** (surrender). Study these words, and you will experience the pleasure of a **BURGEONING** (rapidly expanding) vocabulary and a rising SAT score!

303 | LAMBASTE

Denounce; strongly criticize

Movie critics **EFFUSIVELY** (Word 36) praised the film *Avatar* for its cutting-edge digital special effects. However, the same critics **LAMBASTED** the movie for its **PEDESTRIAN** (Word 296) plot and **PLATITUDINOUS** (Word 36) dialogue. One critic wrote that *Avatar* is "a world to behold and a story to forget."

304 | QUIESCENT

Marked by inactivity; in a state of quiet repose

In CE 79, Pompeii was a prosperous Roman town of 10,000 to 20,000 people. Pompeians planted vineyards and grazed their sheep on the slopes of nearby Mt. Vesuvius. The mountain appeared to be benign and **QUIESCENT**, but looks were deceiving. On August 24, CE 79, Mt. Vesuvius erupted, transforming Pompeii from a lively, crowded city into a ghost town. Modern geologists now know that Mt. Vesuvius is far from **QUIESCENT**. Since three million people now live close to it, it is one of the most potentially dangerous volcanoes in the world.

305 | PROVISIONAL

*Tentative; temporary; for the time being (like a **PROVISIONAL** driver's license)*

Quick: how many planets are there in the Solar System? If you answered nine, you were right up until 2006. From the time of its discovery in 1930 until 2006, Pluto was counted as the Solar System's ninth planet. However, this classification proved to be **PROVISIONAL**. On August 24, 2006, the International Astronomical Union (IAU) reclassified Pluto as a member of a new category of dwarf planets. So now the Solar System contains eight official planets and at least three dwarf planets, including Pluto. Pluto's new status has raised a storm of controversy. Insisting that Pluto should still be a planet, traditionalists have protested the IAU's decision. The controversy has resulted in the **COINING** (Word 289) of a new verb "plutoed." Chosen as the 2006 Word of the Year, "to Pluto" means to demote or devalue someone or something.

306 | LURID
Sensational; shocking; ghastly

During the late 1890s, newspaper publishers, led by William Randolph Hearst and Joseph Pulitzer, attempted to outdo each other with sensational headlines and **LURID** stories about alleged atrocities in Cuba. For example, Hearst's *Journal American* published a **LURID** sketch depicting the disrobing and searching of an American woman by Spanish officials.

The phrase "yellow journalism" was **COINED** (Word 289) to describe tactics employed in the heated competition between the publishers; tactics that became permanent practices of journalists around the world. Recent news events have created even more sensational headlines and **LURID** scandal-mongering.

307 | TRUCULENT, PUGNACIOUS, BELLIGERENT
Defiantly aggressive; eager to fight

On February 15, 1898, the battleship *Maine* mysteriously blew up, causing the loss of 200 sailors in Havana harbor. Led by Theodore Roosevelt, **TRUCULENT** Americans demanded that President McKinley declare war. When the cautious president delayed, the **PUGNACIOUS** Roosevelt reportedly snarled that McKinley had "the backbone of a chocolate éclair." TR's **BELLIGERENT** attitude left no **LATITUDE** (leeway) for compromise.

KNOW YOUR ROOTS		
LATIN ROOT: ***BELLI*** | war	BELLICOSE ANTEBELLUM BELLATRIX REBELLION	fond of war, disposed to quarrel or fight before the war, specifically the American Civil War In ancient Rome a *bellatrix* was a female warrior. Harry Potter fans will recognize *bellum* in the name Bellatrix Lestrange. a renewed war (literally), a defiance of authority or government

308 | PROPITIATE

To appease; to conciliate; to regain the favor or goodwill of

Stung by Roosevelt's barb (see Word 307) and shaken by the public's demand for revenge, President McKinley recognized the inevitable and **PROPITIATED** both Roosevelt and the public. On April 11, 1898, McKinley sent a war message to Congress urging armed intervention to avenge the sinking of the *Maine* and to free oppressed Cubans.

309 | ÉLAN

A vigorous spirit; great enthusiasm

A leader of unbounded energy, Theodore Roosevelt promptly formed a volunteer regiment nicknamed the "Rough Riders" to spearhead the American invasion of Cuba. The Rough Riders included a mixture of cowboys, Ivy League graduates, and star athletes. Although short on discipline, the Rough Riders were long on **ÉLAN**. Dressed in a uniform custom-made by Brooks Brothers, TR demonstrated both courage and **ÉLAN** as he led a victorious charge up San Juan Hill.

310 | PERFUNCTORY

Something performed in a spiritless, mechanical, and routine manner

In her rendition of Rudy Clark's "Shoop Shoop Song (It's In His Kiss)," Cher famously poses this question: "Does he love me, I wanna know, how can I tell if he loves me so?" Cher provides the answer: "If you wanna know if he loves you so, it's in his kiss, that's where it is." So what is the difference between a passionate kiss that proves he loves you and a **PERFUNCTORY** kiss that suggests he doesn't? A passionate kiss is filled with emotion and feeling. In contrast, a **PERFUNCTORY** kiss is a quick routine peck on the cheek. A **PERFUNCTORY** kiss probably means that a relationship is becoming routine and **TEPID** (Word 416).

311 | APLOMB

Self-assurance; confident composure; admirable poise under pressure

On March 4, 1933, over 100,000 Americans gathered around the Capitol building to hear Franklin D. Roosevelt's Inaugural Address. The national mood was as bleak as the grey clouds on that cold Saturday. Faced with plummeting unemployment, falling stock prices, and collapsing banks, the government seemed paralyzed. But FDR was **UNDAUNTED** (Word 73). With his characteristic **APLOMB**, Roosevelt proclaimed: "The only thing we have to fear is fear itself." The President's **APLOMB** lifted the nation's spirit. Witnesses reported that at the end of FDR's speech, the applause was thunderous, rolling like waves across Washington D.C.

312 | OPAQUE

Hard to understand; impenetrably dense and obscure

The following describes a painting entitled *October* by the modern American artist Kenneth Noland:

"*The prototypical Circles, numbering some 175 examples, alone embrace a multitude of moods and means—from propulsive versus sun-drenched hues to those of the type of October, displaying an economy, coolness, and quiddity that almost anticipate a Minimalist aesthetic.***"**

Do you understand what the author is trying to say? Is the writer **LUCID** (clear) or **OPAQUE**? Most editors would probably revise or delete this dense sentence because its **OPACITY** makes it incomprehensible for all but the most knowledgeable readers.

313 | CRAVEN

Cowardly; CONTEMPTIBLY (deserving of scorn) faint-hearted

One of the more shocking aspects of the *News of the World* phone-hacking scandal was the revelation that those who might have exerted some authority, such as police and politicians, did nothing to confront the giant news corporation. The **CRAVEN** behavior of those elected or trusted to look after the public was appalling.

In his book *1940: Myth and Reality*, Clive Ponting asserts, "In the 1930s the British Empire was one of the strongest powers in the world, but through a misguided and **CRAVEN** policy of appeasement and failure to rearm, it allowed the aggressor states (Germany, Italy, and Japan) to expand until war became inevitable."

314 | VENAL

Corrupt; dishonest; open to bribery

Gerald Garson, a **VENAL** former New York Supreme Court Justice, served a prison term from June 2007 to December 2009 for accepting bribes to manipulate the outcomes of divorce proceedings. Garson's acts of **MALFEASANCE** (Word 280) also involved other **VENAL** accomplices. A "fixer" would first find a suitable client and claim to be able to steer the case to a sympathetic judge. The fixer then referred the client to a corrupt lawyer, who bribed Garson with drinks, meals, and money to receive favorable treatment. The fixer would then bribe court employees to assign the client's case to Garson, who would rule in favor of the lawyer.

315 | LICENTIOUS

Immoral; DISSOLUTE; debauched

In his book *The Twelve Caesars*, the Roman historian Suetonious described the **LICENTIOUS** behavior of the first Roman emperors. He particularly **DECRIED** (Word 174) the **DISSOLUTE** antics of Emperor Caligula. When Caligula's grandmother Antonia **ADMONISHED**

(Word 69) him to change his ways, Caligula rebuked her with the remark, "Remember that I have the right to do anything to anybody." Drunk with power, Caligula bathed in perfume, built great pleasure barges, and demanded that he be worshipped as a god. Caligula's **LICENTIOUS** reign came to an abrupt end when one of his guards killed him in a secret passage of the palace. At first, many Romans hesitated to believe the news, fearing that this was a trick of the **DISSOLUTE** emperor to discover who would rejoice at his death.

316 | NOXIOUS

Harmful; injurious to physical, mental, or moral health

China's lax environmental policies and repressive political system are **NOXIOUS** to its citizens' physical and moral well-being. Every night, columns of freight trucks spewing dark clouds of diesel exhaust rumble into China's crowded cities. These **NOXIOUS** fumes are by far China's largest source of street-level pollution. Meanwhile, many claim that China is a **NOXIOUS** one-party state where thousands of its citizens are imprisoned for "crimes" ranging from advocating a multiparty system to using the Internet to call for governmental reform.

317 | SUPERFLUOUS, EXTRANEOUS

Unnecessary; extra

The movie *The Dark Knight* includes a scene in which Batman leaves Gotham City and travels to Hong Kong, marking the first time that Batman has ever left Gotham. While some critics and fans praised this **UNPRECEDENTED** (Word 279) dramatic development, others criticized it as a **SUPERFLUOUS** subplot. One movie critic called it a "pointless jaunt" in an otherwise brilliant movie. What is your opinion? Do you think the Hong Kong scenes were essential to the story or **EXTRANEOUS** scenes that should have been deleted?

Most likely the last time you purchased or rented a DVD or Blu-ray Disc, you saw a menu option for "Special Features" or "Extras." Extras are **SUPERFLUOUS** excerpts that the director decided to share with the public. These **EXTRANEOUS** features can include outtakes, bloopers, deleted scenes, alternate endings, interviews, or director's cut.

KNOW YOUR ROOTS		
LATIN ROOT:		
SUPER, **SUPRA**	over, above, greater in quality	SUPERCILIOUS — overbearing, proud, haughty SUPERFICIAL — on the surface, shallow SUPERLATIVE — the best, in the highest degree SUPERNATURAL — above and beyond all nature SUPERSEDE — to take the place of, to SUPPLANT

318 | DUPLICITOUS

Deliberately deceptive in behavior or speech

What do Ferris Bueller (*Ferris Bueller's Day Off*), Dewey Finn (*School of Rock*), and Frank Abagnale Jr. (*Catch Me if You Can*) have in common? All three are **DUPLICITOUS**, but all three tell lies with great **PANACHE** (Word 81) or flair. Ferris dines at an expensive restaurant while pretending to be Abe Fromer, a Chicago sausage king. Dewey impersonates Ned so that he can take a job as a substitute teacher at a prestigious elementary school. And the 18-year-old Frank convinces Brenda that he is a Harvard graduate, a doctor, and a Lutheran.

319 | PROFLIGATE

Wasteful; SQUANDERING time and money by living for the moment

Hollywood stars tend to be more **PROFLIGATE** than **PARSIMONIOUS** (Word 253). Tom and Katie Cruise's motto seems to be "Spend, spend, spend." Tom owns four private jets, including a $28 million Gulfstream. The Cruises annually spend over $1 million just on fuel for their jaunts around the world. The **PROFLIGATE** couple spares no expense on their daughter Suri, who wears couture clothing and frequently goes on shopping sprees. Tom and Katie built Suri a $100,000 Disney castle-themed playroom in their mansion. Suri has **EXORBITANT** (Word 162) birthday parties, and Tom added $5 million to her trust fund as a gift for her fifth birthday.

320 | EPIPHANY

A sudden realization; an insightful moment

Have you ever performed in a school play? For most students, acting in a school play is a great way to meet people and have fun. But for a few student-actors, it can be a life-changing experience. For example, when Leighton Meester was just 11, she performed in her school play *The Wizard of Oz*. As she was performing, Leighton had an **EPIPHANY**: "I realized acting was what I wanted to do." Leighton turned her **EPIPHANY** into reality. Today she plays Blair Waldorf in the popular television program *Gossip Girl*.

321 | INSIDIOUS

Causing harm in a subtle or stealthy manner; devious

In *The Scarlet Letter*, Roger Chillingworth is Hester Prynne's long-absent husband. He returns to Boston to find that Hester has had an affair with an unknown man and is now the mother of an illegitimate daughter. Consumed with vengefulness, Chillingworth vows to find and then psychologically torture Hester's secret lover. Sensing a hidden guilt, Chillingworth soon launches an **INSIDIOUS** plan to torment the Reverend Arthur Dimmesdale.

322 | VACUOUS, INANE

Empty; lacking serious purpose; VAPID

On the TV show *Glee*, Brittany is a **VACUOUS** cheerleader who is prone to making **INANE** comments. For example, Brittany responded to her teacher's question "What is a capital of Ohio?" by answering, "O." But no one could accuse Brittany of creating the "Glist List" of school hotties because, as she admitted, "I don't know how to turn on a computer."

323 | HARBINGER, PORTENT, PRESAGE

Indications or omens that something important or calamitous is about to occur

Recent scientific studies have confirmed that the North Pole is melting. This startling fact **PRESAGES** difficult times for polar bears and other Arctic animals that rely on sea ice to survive. It is also a **HARBINGER** of coming trouble for humans. The melting ice will raise sea levels, thus posing a threat to coastal cities and villages. Alarmed scientists are warning world leaders that these **PORTENTS** should not be ignored. They are calling for international **ACCORDS** (Word 256) to **ARREST** (Word 281) the rise in carbon dioxide emissions.

324 | BELEAGUER

To beset; to surround with problems

In the movie *Remember the Titans*, Herman Boone, a successful black football coach from North Carolina, is hired to replace the popular white coach Bill Yoast at newly integrated T.C. Williams High School in Alexandria, Virginia. Boone is immediately **BELEAGUERED** by a host of problems. Outraged by his demotion, Yoast threatens to resign. At the same time, tensions quickly erupt between black and white members of the football team. These tensions reflect the turmoil in Alexandria, where extremists resent Coach Boone and demand that he resign.

325 | BURGEON

To grow rapidly; to expand

Although **BELEAGUERED** (see Word 324) by seemingly **INSUR-MOUNTABLE** (Word 185) problems, Coach Boone proves to be **RESOLUTE** (Word 352) and resourceful. He **ADROITLY** (Word 67) unifies both his coaching staff and his team. Once they learn to work together, the Titans win victory after victory. Community support soon **BURGEONS** as the town and school rally behind their victorious and unified football team.

326 | IMPERIOUS

Domineering and arrogant; haughty

What do the Persian ruler Xerxes, the English King Henry VIII, and the French king Louis XIV have in common? All three were **IMPERIOUS** leaders. Xerxes **IMPERIOUSLY** insisted that his subjects all bow down before their god-king. Henry VIII **IMPERIOUSLY** demanded obedience from his subjects and his wives. Louis XIV **IMPERIOUSLY** (but truthfully) asserted that in France, "L'État, c'est moi," meaning "The State is me."

327 | PETULANT

Peevish, irritable

Britney Spears is notorious for her **PETULANT** behavior. For example, just an hour before going on stage at the MTV Video Music Awards, Britney **PETULANTLY** insisted on doing her own hair. She abruptly told her hair stylist, "You're really annoying me. Get out!" That the **PETULANT** Pop Princess ended up doing her own hair proved to be a **FIASCO** (Word 146).

328 | COMPLAISANT

Agreeable; marked by a pleasing personality; AFFABLE; AMIABLE (Word 18)

Tip for a Direct Hit

Although COMPLAISANT and complacent sound alike, they are two very different words. Complacent has come to have pejorative nuances. It means over-contented, smug, and self-satisfied. In contrast, COMPLAISANT is derived from the prefix *com*, meaning "with," and the root *plaisir*, meaning "pleasure." So COMPLAISANT literally means "with pleasure" and thus describes a person who does things "with pleasure."

Compare Britney Spears with Giselle, the fairy tale princess, in the movie *Enchanted*. While Britney is **PETULANT** (Word 305) and peevish, Giselle exudes a natural goodness that delights both humans and animals. Her **COMPLAISANT** personality even charms **NOTORIOUSLY** (widely but unfavorably known) ill-tempered New Yorkers who stop what they are doing to spontaneously sing and dance with the ever-**AFFABLE** (Word 18) Giselle.

329 | FAWN

*Behaving in a **SERVILE**, **OBSEQUIOUS** (Word 364), or **SUBSERVIENT** manner*

In *300*, Xerxes promises Leonidas great wealth and power. All the Spartan king has to do is kneel before the Persian god-king. But Leonidas is a proud Spartan who refuses to act in a **FAWNING** manner toward anyone. Leonidas rebuffs Xerxes, saying, "Kneeling will be hard for me. I'm afraid killing all those slaves of yours has left me with a nasty cramp in my leg."

Waylon Smithers of *The Simpsons* is the **SUBSERVIENT** assistant to Mr. Burns at Springfield Nuclear Power Plant. Smithers is constantly **FAWNING** over his boss, willing to attend to Mr. Burns's every whim and fancy. In one instance, Mr. Burns is relaxing in his hot tub while Smithers cleans his back with a sponge, when the following conversation takes place:

Mr. Burns: *Careful, Smithers, that sponge has corners, you know.*

Smithers: [**FAWNING**] *I'll go find a spherical one, sir.*

330 | OBDURATE, INTRANSIGENT

*Very stubborn; obstinate; unyieldingly persistent; inflexible; **INTRACTABLE***

What do the Spartan leader King Leonidas and President Woodrow Wilson have in common? They were both very **OBDURATE**. In the movie *300*, Leonidas **OBDURATELY** insisted, "The battle is over when I say it is over. No surrender. No retreat." Similarly, Wilson **OBDURATELY** refused to accept any of Senator Lodge's reservations that would modify the League of Nations. The **INTRANSIGENT** Wilson insisted, "I shall consent to nothing."

331 | REDOLENT

Exuding fragrance; full of a specified smell; suggestive of; reminiscent

In her Harry Potter series, author J.K. Rowling often describes how the **REDOLENT** fragrance of a particularly delicious feast would **WAFT** (float) across the Great Hall at Hogwarts. In William Faulkner's novels of the American South, a fragrance **REDOLENT** of magnolia blooms and the Antebellum era seems to **WAFT** from the pages.

332 | CHICANERY
Deception by subterfuge; deliberate trickery

In her book, *Century of Dishonor*, Helen Hunt Jackson exposed the American government's **CHICANERY** in deliberately cheating the Native Americans. For example, Jackson sharply criticized government officials for their **CHICANERY** in signing treaties they had no intention of honoring.

Are you familiar with a type of computer program called a Trojan horse? The name of this destructive software comes from the famous act of **CHICANERY** performed by the Greeks in the Trojan War. Today, a Trojan horse is a program that pretends to perform some desirable function, such as providing a new screen saver. Instead, once inside your computer, a Trojan horse will perform destructive acts of **CHICANERY**, such as stealing data, downloading malware, or crashing the hard drive.

333 | CONUNDRUM
A difficult problem; a dilemma with no easy solution

In the movie *Knocked Up*, slacker Ben Stone and ambitious, career-minded Allison Scott meet at a local night club and then spend the night together. The following morning, they quickly discover that they have little in common. Eight weeks later, Allison is shocked to discover that she is pregnant. She then contacts the equally-shocked Ben to tell him the news. Allison and Ben now face a difficult **CONUNDRUM**. Will Allison choose to be a single mother, or will she and Ben give their relationship a chance?

334 | SLIGHT

To treat as unimportant; to deliberately ignore; to disrespect

On April 29, 2011, as the world watched the wedding of Prince William and Kate Middleton, one very prominent royal was not in attendance at Westminster Abbey. In fact, she wasn't even invited! The royal family **SLIGHTED** Sarah Ferguson, Duchess of York, the former wife of Prince Andrew by declining to invite her to her nephew's nuptials. The year before, the Duchess of York had been caught attempting to sell access to the royal family to a reporter. In response, she was not invited to the wedding, even though her daughters and former husband were. The Duchess of York later said she had really wanted to attend the wedding with her family and that the **SLIGHT** was really difficult to deal with.

335 | CAPITULATE

To surrender; to comply without protest

What do the King Leonidas and General George Washington have in common? Both refused to **CAPITULATE** when faced with certain defeat. In the movie *300*, King Leonidas refused to **CAPITULATE** to the Persians when he defiantly insisted, "Spartans never surrender. Spartans never retreat." Similarly, George Washington refused to **CAPITULATE** when the British and Hessians had apparently trapped his army on the Pennsylvania side of the Delaware River. Defiantly **EXHORTING** (Word 53) his troops, "Victory or Death!", Washington boldly crossed the ice-filled Delaware on Christmas Eve and surprised the Hessians at Trenton.

336 | DISHEARTENING

Very discouraging; dismaying; dispiriting

What do Samuel Tilden and Al Gore have in common? Both men were Democratic presidential candidates who won the popular vote but suffered **DISHEARTENING** defeats in the Electoral College. Tilden lost the controversial 1876 election, and Gore lost the hotly disputed 2000 election. However, both men overcame their **DISHEARTENING** defeats. Tilden became a major benefactor of the New York Public Library, and Gore has become one of the world's foremost environmental activists.

337 | APOCRYPHAL
Of doubtful authenticity; false; SPURIOUS

American students have long been taught that the Spanish explorer Ponce de Leon discovered Florida while searching for the Fountain of Youth. The story is **APOCRYPHAL**. While Ponce de Leon did discover Florida, there is no evidence that he was searching for the Fountain of Youth. Like other Spanish conquistadores, he was searching for gold and new lands to expand the Spanish Empire.

The Apocrypha is the name given to various writings that have been kept out of the Bible as not genuine. The Shakespeare Apocrypha is a collection of 14 plays that have been ascribed to Shakespeare over the years but have been entitled **SPURIOUS** and *Doubtful*.

338 | MAGISTERIAL
Learned and authoritative

In England, a magistrate was a royal official entrusted with the administration of the laws. Magistrates naturally wanted to appear **MAGISTERIAL** or learned and authoritative. In the movie *The Wizard of Oz*, the Munchkin mayor wants to appear **MAGISTERIAL** when he grandly welcomes Dorothy by publicly proclaiming, "As Mayor of the Munchkin City in the County of the Land of Oz, I welcome you most regally." Then he **MAGISTERIALLY** announces that the Wicked Witch is "Positively, absolutely, undeniably, and reliably dead."

339 | PLASTIC, MALLEABLE, PLIABLE

Flexible; easily shaped, especially by outside influences or forces

The 17th century English philosopher John Locke argued that at birth the human mind is a blank tablet (*tabula rasa*) and that, as a result, all of our ideas are shaped by experience. Locke thus believed that humans are by nature **MALLEABLE**. Modern public relations specialists have extended Locke's view to include the belief that public opinion is also highly **PLASTIC** and can therefore be shaped. For example, in the movie *Hancock*, Hancock is a **SURLY** (Word 385) superhero who is so disliked that most people in Los Angeles want him to leave their city. However, Ray Embrey is a public relations specialist who is determined to transform Hancock's image. Embrey's faith in the **PLASTICITY** of public opinion proves to be justified. Popular attitudes prove to be **PLIABLE** when Hancock becomes a popular hero after he saves a policeman's life.

340 | CHAGRIN

The feeling of distress caused by humiliation, failure, or embarrassment

In the movie *Anchorman*, Brian Fantana discovers to his **CHAGRIN** that his cologne is so foul-smelling that it repels Veronica and everyone else in the newsroom. In the movie *Pretty Woman*, Vivian is deeply **CHAGRINED** when **SUPERCILIOUS** (Word 395) clerks in a fashionable clothing store refuse to help her because of the way she is dressed.

341 | OBSTREPEROUS

Noisily and stubbornly defiant; unruly; boisterous

The television program *Supernanny* features Jo Frost's amazing ability to tame even the wildest and most **OBSTREPEROUS** children. The hit reality show *Toddlers and Tiaras* focuses on young girls who compete in beauty pageants. Most of the children on the show are **OBSTREPEROUS**. They scream, cry, and yell at their parents, and several of them have even slapped their mothers. Many of the parents on the show could use help from the Supernanny to discipline their **OBSTREPEROUS** pageant girls.

342 | IDYLLIC
Charmingly simple and carefree

What do Happy Land in *Happy Gilmore* and Andalasia in *Enchanted* have in common? Both are charming, **IDYLLIC** places. Happy Land is an imaginary place where Happy can relax with Virginia and forget about Shooter McGavin. Andalasia is an **IDYLLIC** paradise where magical creatures and humans all live carefree, blissful lives.

343 | DILAPIDATED
Having fallen into a state of disrepair; broken-down; in deplorable condition

In his autobiography *Black Boy*, Richard Wright provides a vivid description of the nightmare of living in a **DILAPIDATED** home furnished with broken furniture and filthy kitchen appliances. President Johnson's Great Society included urban renewal projects designed to rebuild **DILAPIDATED** neighborhoods like the one Richard Wright lived in.

344 | EXTEMPORIZE, IMPROVISE
To lecture or speak without notes

Dr. King's "I Have a Dream" speech is one of the most **ACCLAIMED** (Word 91) orations in American history. Yet most people are unaware that Dr. King **EXTEMPORIZED** most of the speech. After beginning with his prepared text, Dr. King **IMPROVISED**, saying, "We will not be satisfied until justice runs down like waters and righteousness like a mighty stream." Knowing that Dr. King had wandered from his prepared text, the renowned gospel singer Mahalia Jackson urged him to continue by shouting out, "Tell 'em about the dream, Martin." Dr. King then began the **EXTEMPORIZED** "Dream" sequence that **GALVANIZED** (Word 148) his audience and inspired the nation.

345 | MYRIAD

Many; numerous

In *Harry Potter and the Half-Blood Prince*, **MYRIAD** problems test Harry during his sixth year at Hogwarts. Harry's challenges include retrieving a key memory from Professor Slughorn, dealing with his romantic feelings for Ginny, helping Professor Dumbledore destroy Lord Voldemort's Horcruxes, and **THWARTING** (Word 67) Draco Malfoy's sinister scheme. Harry must draw upon all of his skills as a wizard to successfully meet the demands posed by these **MYRIAD** tasks.

346 | UNGAINLY

Awkward; clumsy; NOT graceful

What do Mia Thermopolis (*The Princess Diaries*) and Jess Day (*New Girl*) have in common? Both are **AFFABLE** (Word 18) but **UNGAINLY** young women. Mia is the 15-year-old heir to the throne of the fictional kingdom of Genovia. She attends an exclusive private school and is regularly teased by her peers for her **UNGAINLY** manner and frizzy hair. She takes etiquette lessons called "Princess Lessions" to help her become more graceful and self-assured in her new royal role.

Jess is a charming but awkward young woman who moves in with three guy roommates after breaking up with her boyfriend. She considers denim overalls to be appropriate attire for a first date, and she frequently bursts into song for no reason. She is **UNGAINLY** in social situations, so her new roommates try to help her become less awkward.

347 | DILATORY
Habitually late; tardy

With SAT scores, transcripts, applications, essays, and recommendation letters, there's a lot for students to keep track of during their senior year. As they try to balance their schoolwork and extracurricular activities with their college applications, they tend to be **DILATORY** when it comes to the enormous task of writing their college essays. This **DILATORY** behavior is a major **BANE** (Word 16) of college counselors, who must **IMPLORE** (urge) them to finish their essays in a timely manner. Even though writing college essays is a **DAUNTING** (intimidating) task, actually submitting the applications is a **BOON** (Word 16) to students and their anxious parents, who can finally relax again. We **EXHORT** (Word 53) you not to be **DILATORY**; instead, finish up your college applications quickly!

348 | VITUPERATIVE
Characterized by verbal abuse and bitter criticism

Most critics have panned the Adam Sandler movie *Jack and Jill*, calling it one of his worst yet. One of Hollywood's most successful actors and blessed with a loyal fanbase, he can still fill the seats, but that did not stop critics from being amazingly **VITUPERATIVE**. Here are some of the **VITUPERATIVE** reviews:

- Just in time for Thanksgiving, Adam Sandler has released his biggest turkey yet.

- A father now in real life, it's as if he feels obligated to put heart-warming messages in his films, even if they feel **DISINGENUOUS** (Word 419).

- I don't think that all of Sandler's comedies warrant shame, but this one is a disgrace.

- In *Jack and Jill*, the biggest joke of all is on you.

349 | DISCORDANT

Not in harmony; incompatible; at variance with, as in a DISCORDANT detail that doesn't fit a pattern

In *The Cornish Trilogy*, Francis Cornish is an art expert who specializes in finding **DISCORDANT** details to prove that a painting is not authentic. Cornish demonstrates his amazing powers of observation and command of **ESOTERIC** (Word 394) facts when he evaluates a painting thought to be by the 15th century Dutch master Hubert van Eyck. The painting includes a monkey hanging by its tail from the bars of Hell. This seemingly **INNOCUOUS** (Word 99) image proves to be a **DISCORDANT** detail. Monkeys with prehensile tails did not exist in Europe until the 16th century. Since van Eyck died in 1426, the painting has to be a forgery!

350 | PERFIDIOUS

Treacherous; traitorous; deceitful

What do Judas Iscariot, Ephialtes, Benedict Arnold, and Peter Pettigrew have in common? All four were **PERFIDIOUS** traitors and opportunists. Judas betrayed Christ, Ephialtes betrayed the Spartans, Benedict Arnold betrayed the Colonial Army, and Peter Pettigrew ("Wormtail") betrayed James and Lily Potter.

351 | PROLIFERATE

To increase rapidly

Pop and rap have traditionally been separate musical genres. But that **DICHOTOMY** (division into contrasting parts) is disappearing. There is now a **PROLIFERATION** of songs that blend rapping and singing. Often, singers will collaborate with rappers on their songs. For example, Katy Perry's hit "California Gurls" features Snoop Dogg, and Justin Bieber's "Baby" features a rap by Ludacris. Enrique Iglesias has featured rappers Pitbull and Ludacris on his latest singles. There is also a **PROLIFERATION** of artists who are talented at both singing and rapping. Ke$ha has created her signature combination of singing and rapping, and rapper Nicki Minaj displays her incredible vocal range on her hit song "Super Bass."

352 | INDOMITABLE, RESOLUTE

Very determined; unwavering

The Buffalo Bills' tight end Kevin Everett suffered a severe spinal cord injury while making a tackle in the opening game of the 2007 NFL season. Everett was paralyzed from the neck down when he arrived at the hospital. Doctors feared that Everett would never walk again. But Everett remained **RESOLUTE**. State-of-the-art medical care and his own **INDOMITABLE** spirit gave Everett the will to fight every day for recovery. Remarkably, Everett is now able to walk again. His courage and **RESOLUTE** attitude have inspired others who have suffered similar injuries.

353 | MORIBUND

Approaching death; about to become OBSOLETE (Word 25)

Tip for a Direct Hit

The Latin noun *mors*, meaning "death" is also seen in MOROSE (Word 27) and MORBID, both of which mean depressed and preoccupied with death. A person who is MORTIFIED is figuratively "dying from embarrassment." Lord Voldemort's name means "flight from death."

As the year CE 476 began, the once invincible Roman Empire was a **MORIBUND** remnant of its once-great self. Germanic tribes overran its western provinces, while the Ostrogoths invaded Italy. After Rome was sacked by the Vandals in CE 455, the city's broken aqueducts, shattered monuments, and looted temples were mere shadows of their former glory. The last Roman emperor was a 14-year-old boy whose name, Romulus Augustulus, recalled 1000 years of past grandeur. Recognizing that the emperor was powerless and that his empire was MORIBUND, a barbarian general named Odoacer dismissed the boy emperor, thus finalizing "the fall of the Roman Empire."

354 | NUANCE

*A **SUBTLE** (Word 96) shade of meaning or feeling; a slight degree of difference*

In the movie *Harry Potter and the Half-Blood Prince*, actor Tom Felton portrays Draco Malfoy. The role requires a **NUANCED** performance. When Lord Voldemort assigns him the mission of killing Albus Dumbledore, Draco feels conflicted. He is torn between his ambition to please Voldemort and a fear of committing a heinous crime he might always regret. Felton relished the opportunity to portray Draco's **NUANCED** emotions. "If you're feeling sorry for him," says Felton, "then I've done my job."

355 | FLIPPANT, FACETIOUS

Treating serious matters with lighthearted humor or lack of respect

Mark Twain is famous for his **WRY** (Word 6) wit and humorous perspectives on various situations. His masterpiece *The Adventures of Huckleberry Finn* opens with this clever epigraph: "Persons attempting to find a motive in this narrative will be prosecuted; persons attempting to find a moral in it will be banished; persons attempting to find a plot in it will be shot." The **FACETIOUS** epigraph informs the reader that there will, in fact, be serious issues and morals within the novel.

356 | CREDULOUS

*Easily convinced; tending to believe too readily; **GULLIBLE***

INCREDULOUS

*Disbelieving, **SKEPTICAL** (Word 102)*

In his famous *Histories*, the ancient Greek historian Herodotus set out to record "wondrous deeds and wars." Herodotus enlivened his pages with fascinating **ANECDOTES** (Word 233) and illustrations. However, Herodotus was at times overly **CREDULOUS**. For example, he readily accepted reports of giant ants that hoarded gold. Although normally not known for being **CREDULOUS**, Alexander the Great conducted a **FUTILE** (Word 46) search in India for the "gold-digging" ants and their treasure-filled anthills.

In another **ANDECDOTE**, Herodotus claimed that for the second invasion of Greece Xerxes had 2.5 million military personnel accompanied by an equivalent number of support personnel. Modern historians have been **INCREDULOUS** at the numbers given by Herodotus. Most have attributed the numbers to miscalculation or exaggeration by the victors.

357 | FLORID

Flowery in style; very ORNATE (Word 388)

Romance novels are well known for their **FLORID** prose. Written by Stephanie Meyer, *Twilight* is a popular vampire-romance novel that features **FLORID** descriptions. Here is a particularly **FLORID** portrait of Edward Cullen: "He lay perfectly still in the grass, his shirt open over his sculpted, incandescent chest, his **SCINTILLATING** (Word 407) arms bare. His glistening, pale lavender lids were shut, though of course he didn't sleep." When Edward opened his eyes, he looked at Bella "with a **WISTFUL** (Word 201) expression. The golden eyes held mine, and I lost my train of thought."

358 | EXCORIATING, SCATHING

Expressing strong disapproval; condemning; loudly DECRYING (Word 174)

On July 8, 2010, LeBron James used a nationally televised interview to announce his decision to leave the Cleveland Cavaliers and play basketball for the Miami Heat. While jubilant Miami fans celebrated, Cavalier owner Dan Gilbert issued a **SCATHING** statement **EXCORIATING** James for his "cowardly betrayal." The **APOPLECTIC** (furious, enraged) owner guaranteed that the Cavaliers would win an NBA Championship before the self-styled former king won one.

359 | INTERLOPER

An intruder; a gatecrasher

In the movie *Wedding Crashers*, Owen Wilson and Vince Vaughn star as a pair of Washington divorce mediators who spend their spring weekends crashing weddings. The two charming **INTERLOPERS** always concoct clever back stories to deceive inquisitive guests. After a successful season, the pair of **INTERLOPERS** infiltrate a particularly **LAVISH** (Word 388) wedding where Owen unexpectedly falls for one of the bridesmaids.

360 | CEREBRAL

Intellectual rather than emotional

VISCERAL

Instinctive rather than rational

Tip for a Direct Hit

The words CEREBRAL and VISCERAL are both derived from parts of the human body. The cerebrum is the main part of the human brain and is associated with thought. Viscera are soft internal organs and thus are associated with internal or "gut" feelings.

Do you typically follow your head or your heart? If you follow your head, you have a **CEREBRAL** or intellectual response to problems. In contrast, if you follow your heart, then you have a **VISCERAL** or emotional response to problems. The Star Trek movies vividly depict this age-old duality. Spock is a **CEREBRAL** science officer whose decisions are governed by logic. In contrast, Dr. McCoy is a physician whose decisions are often affected by his gut reactions to a situation.

361 | NONPLUSSED, CONFOUNDED

Utterly PERPLEXED (Word 19); completely puzzled; totally bewildered

On July 14, 1789, a mob successfully stormed a royal fortress in Paris known as the Bastille. The rioters overpowered the guards and seized 20,000 pounds of gunpowder. While these **MOMENTOUS** (Word 193) events were taking place, King Louis XVI spent an uneventful day hunting. The exhausted monarch returned to the palace at Versailles and went to sleep. The Duc de La Rochefoucauld-Liancourt awakened the sleepy king and reported what had happened at the Bastille. The shocking report left Louis **CONFOUNDED**. Confused and at a loss for words, Louis finally stammered, "Is this a rebellion?" The Duc emphatically replied, "No, sire, it is a revolution."

362 | IGNOMINIOUS
Humiliating; shameful; disgraceful

Almost a billion people watched Spain defeat the Netherlands 1–0 to capture the 2010 World Cup. The Spanish victory ignited joyous celebrations across Spain. While the triumphant Spanish team received a hero's welcome, the French team returned home in a cargo plane. Furious French soccer fans demanded answers for their team's humiliating failure to win a single match. France's **IGNOMINIOUS** early exit left the soccer-crazed nation in shock and anger. The nation's leading sports newspaper called the **DEBACLE** (Word 146) "a state scandal."

363 | EUPHONY
Soothing or pleasant sounds; harmony

CACOPHONY
Harsh, clashing, jarring, grating sounds; disharmony

Tip for a Direct Hit

EUPHONY and CACOPHONY both include the Greek root PHONE meaning "sound" (like a cell phone). Since the prefix *EU* means "good," EUPHONY literally means "good sound." Since the prefix *KAKOS* means "bad," CACOPHONY means "bad sound."

In their classic Motown song, "My Girl," The Temptations tell everyone who will listen: "I've got a sweeter song than the birds in the trees. Well, I guess you'd say, what can make me feel this way? My girl, talkin' 'bout my girl." The Temptations' soothing words and harmonious melody create a **EUPHONIOUS** sound. In contrast, rapper Eminem describes his apprehension and fear before a make-or-break performance: "His palms are sweaty, knees weak, arms heavy. There's vomit on his sweater already, mom's spaghetti." Eminem's harsh grating words and rapid-fire rhythm create a **CACOPHONOUS** sound.

364 | OBSEQUIOUS

Promptly obedient, submissive; marked by or exhibiting FAWNING (Word329) attentiveness

Among the most **OBSEQUIOUS** characters in literature are Rosencrantz and Guildenstern, Hamlet's childhood acquaintances, who at King Claudius's **BEHEST** (bidding, command) attempt to learn why Hamlet is behaving strangely. They fall over themselves **DEFERRING** (yielding) to Hamlet, agreeing with him, **FAWNING** over him. Hamlet is not fooled by their **DUPLICITY** (Word 318).

365 | TIMOROUS

Showing nervousness or fear

In the movie *Ferris Bueller's Day Off*, Cameron Frye is Ferris's **TIMOROUS** best friend. Cameron lacks the sheer confidence and carefree attitude of Ferris. Whereas Ferris enjoys skipping school to go on adventures, Cameron worries about the consequences. He fears getting caught by Principal Rooney and is especially **TIMOROUS** in dealing with his authoritative father. However, Cameron eventually enjoys their day off and decides to face his fears and stand up to his father.

CHAPTER 11

The Toughest Words II | *366 – 430*

Chapter 11 continues with 65 of the toughest words on the SAT. As in Chapter 10, each of these words was the answer or answer choice to a Level 5 question. You'll find that we have used an **ECLECTIC** (diverse) mix of popular and historic examples to help **ELUCIDATE** (clarify, explain) the meaning of each word. Don't be **CHURLISH** (ill-tempered) or **REFRACTORY** (obstinate). Our **SCINTILLATING** (sparkling) examples will inspire you to complete the final 65 words. When you finish, you'll be an articulate student who can write forcefully, speak eloquently, and achieve soaring scores on the SAT!

366 | IDIOSYNCRASY

A trait or mannerism that is peculiar to an individual

The cast of MTV's *Jersey Shore* all have distinctive **IDIOSYNCRASIES**. For example, Sammi "Sweetheart" loves to wear hair extensions, Vinnie loves to fist pump on the dance floor, Michael "The Situation" loves to show off his chiseled abs, and Pauly D loves to use hair gel. Pauly D spends 30 minutes in the morning and another 30 minutes in the evening sculpting his signature blowout hairstyle. Pauly spends $100 a week on hair gel. Believe it or not, you can go to a hair salon and ask for a "Pauly D" haircut.

367 | CENSORIOUS, CAPTIOUS

Highly critical; fault-finding

In the movie *Animal House*, the Deltas are a group of **BOORISH** (Word 64) fraternity brothers who have done their best to provoke the **CENSORIOUS** Dean of Students, Vernon Wormer. Realizing that for the Deltas, "party animals" is really a **EUPHEMISM** (an inoffensive word substituted for an offensive word) for "drunken students" the outraged dean vows to expel the Deltas from Faber College. Led by "Otter" and "Boon," the **HEDONISTIC** (Word 104) Deltas continue to infuriate their **CAPTIOUS** Dean, who then puts the Deltas on "double secret probation." When the Deltas all fail their midterms, Dean Wormer expels them from school and happily notifies their draft boards of their eligibility. **UNDAUNTED** (Word 73), the Deltas seek revenge by wreaking havoc on Faber College's annual Homecoming parade.

368 | CONSTERNATION

A state of great dismay and confusion

In the movie *Juno*, Juno MacGuff faces many difficult choices. After deciding against getting an abortion, Juno agrees to have a closed adoption with Vanessa and Mark Loring. The Lorings seem like the perfect couple because they are young and **AFFLUENT** (Word 251), and Vanessa has her heart set on becoming a mother. With everything seemingly agreed upon, Juno reacts with great **CONSTERNATION** when Mark later tells her that he has decided to leave Vanessa. Juno ultimately overcomes her **CONSTERNATION** and stands by her agreement to give her baby to Vanessa.

369 | DIDACTIC

Tending to give instruction or advice; inclined to teach or lecture others too much; containing a political or moral lesson

Reformers of American education are advocating a move away from traditional, teacher-centered, **DIDACTIC** instruction where students are passive receptors of knowledge. They support more student-centered teaching that focuses on experimentation and discovery.

DIDACTIC literature aims to teach a moral or religious lesson. Harriet Beecher Stowe's 1852 novel, *Uncle Tom's Cabin*, traces the passage of the slave Uncle Tom through the hands of three owners, ending with the **INFAMOUS** (widely but unfavorably known) Simon Legree. Though the book is often viewed as a **DIDACTIC** abolitionist tract, many critics see the work as far more complex.

The word **DIDACTIC** has come to have **PEJORATIVE** (negative) connotations. Most of us find it irritating to be lectured in ways that are preachy, **PEDANTIC** (tediously **OSTENTATIOUS** (Word 404) about one's knowledge), or **DOGMATIC** (asserting opinions in an authoritative, arrogant manner).

370 | ELUCIDATE

To make clear or plain, especially by explanation

In the movie *Dead Poets Society*, John Keating rejects the textbook's lifeless approach to poetry. Instead, he **ELUCIDATES** an entirely different approach by explaining, "We don't read and write poetry because it's cute. We read and write poetry because we are members of the human race. And the race is filled with passion."

KNOW YOUR ROOTS		
LATIN ROOT: *LUC* | to light, shine	LUCID	lit up, clear, easily understood
	PELLUCID	clear, transparent, DIAPHANOUS, LIMPID
	TRANSLUCENT	shining through, but with diffused light, partially transparent
	LUCITE	a crystal-clear synthetic resin
	LUCIFER	the Fallen Angel, who was the light-bearer to God before defying God and being cast into Hell (In Milton's *Paradise Lost*)

371 | EFFUSIVE

Expressing excessive emotion in an unrestrained manner; gushing

Movie critics are normally restrained and hard-to-please. However, critics have been overwhelmingly **EFFUSIVE** in their praise for Christopher Nolan's work as the director of *The Dark Knight*. Praising the film as "an **EPIC** (Word 231) masterpiece" and "quite possibly the best superhero movie ever made," critics have **LAUDED** (Word 91) Nolan for superbly crafted scenes that include innovative sequences shot using IMAX cameras and breathtaking **VERTIGINOUS** (Word 393) mid-air escapes. Reviewers have not limited their **EFFUSIVE** praise to Nolan's **ADROIT** (Word 68) cinematic techniques. They have also commended his ability to create complex characters that embody the moral **AMBIGUITIES** (Word 21) of a city with a constant tension between good and evil.

372 | PROLIFIC

Very productive

What do the British novelist J. K. Rowling and the American rapper Lil Wayne have in common? At first glance, this may seem like an odd **JUXTAPOSITION** (Word 426). However, both Rowling and Lil Wayne are very successful, popular, and **PROLIFIC**. Rowling's seven-volume **SAGA** (Word 231) contains over 4000 pages. Lil Wayne is a prolific rapper who recorded his first hit when he was just 15. *Rolling Stone* magazine calls the rap megastar "a 24-hour-a-day recording machine."

373 | FUROR

A general commotion; an uproar

In March 2009 AIG announced that the insurance company would be paying out $165 million in executive bonuses. Normally this news would have merited little public notice, but AIG had received $185 billion from American taxpayers to cover the company's enormous losses. The bonuses ignited widespread public **FUROR**. Irate taxpayers deluged Congress with emails and phone calls **LAMBASTING** (Word 303) AIG. Senator Shelby of Alabama articulated the public **FUROR** when he said, "These people brought this on themselves. Now you're rewarding failure. A lot of these people should be fired, not awarded bonuses. This is horrible. It's outrageous."

374 | PARANOIA

A tendency toward excessive or irrational suspiciousness; irrational fear; delusions of persecution

Do you have any irrational fears? If so, you are not alone. Many celebrities have confessed to being **PARANOID** about a variety of everyday things. For example, Cameron Diaz refuses to touch door handles with her bare hands. Although Daniel Radcliffe may play the world's most popular wizard, he has a **PARANOID** reaction to clowns. Johnny Depp and P. Diddy also share Radcliffe's **PARANOIA** about circus entertainers.

375 | MARGINAL, PERIPHERAL

Of secondary importance; NOT central; on the perimeter

Tip for a Direct Hit

MARGINAL gives us the word MARGINALIZE, which means to relegate to a position of secondary or PERIPHERAL importance.

Everyone agrees that Harry, Hermione, and Ron are central characters in the Harry Potter **SAGA** (Word 231). But can you identify Hannah Abbott? Probably not. Hannah was a **MARGINAL** character who was a member of Hufflepuff and Dumbledore's Army. As an adult, she became the wife of Neville Longbottom and the landlady of the Leaky Cauldron.

376 | OBFUSCATE

To deliberately confuse; to make something so confusing that it is hard to understand

The world has been shocked as details of the British tabloid *News of the World*'s phone hacking and press intrusion scandal continue to come to light. The executives have been accused of deliberate **OBFUSCATION** in their handling of the situation by insisting that only a few at the paper knew and took part in the phone-hacking and bribing of British police officers. When the situation escalated into a full-blown scandal, the **VENERABLE** (respected) 168-year-old paper was forced to shut down.

OBFUSCATION is also used in the world of technology. If a programmer wants to write computer applications in JavaScript but doesn't want other users to be able to read, reuse, or reverse-engineer the code, then **OBFUSCATION** can make the reverse-engineering so tedious that it's not worth the effort.

377 | FLUMMOX

To confuse or perplex; utterly dumbfounded

What do viewers of the television series *Lost* and the movie *The Matrix* and its sequels have in common? Both series have complicated and **CRYPTIC** (Word 95) plots that leave many viewers **FLUMMOXED**.

You don't need complicated plots to confuse someone; seemingly **INNOCUOUS** (Word 99) questions have **FLUMMOXED** veteran politicians during interviews or debates. These **GAFFES** (unintentional remarks which cause embarrassment) leave an **INDELIBLE** (not able to be forgotten or removed) impression on voters that have **DELETERIOUS** (Word 173) consequences to their campaigns.

378 | SPATE
A large number or amount

Each year, moviegoers eagerly await the arrival of new blockbuster films with dazzling special effects and riveting action sequences. In the summer of 2011 Hollywood did not disappoint action-adventure fans. Studios produced a **SPATE** of popular super hero films, including *Thor*, *The Green Lantern*, and *Captain America: The First Avenger*. Hollywood also released a **SPATE** of sequels of some of the most popular action film franchises, including *Transformers: Dark of the Moon*, *X-Men: First Class*, *Pirates of the Caribbean: On Stranger Tides*, and *Harry Potter and the Deathly Hallows: Part II*.

379 | INEFFABLE
Too overwhelming to be put into words; indescribable; inexpressible

What do Josie (*Never Been Kissed*) and Giselle (*Enchanted*) have in common? Both experienced a special and thus **INEFFABLE** first kiss. Josie's **INEFFABLE** moment occurred when Mr. Coulson kissed her on the pitcher's mound in front of most of the student body. Giselle's **INEFFABLE** moment occurred when she shared true love's first kiss with Prince Edward.

380 | HISTRIONIC, OVERWROUGHT
Excessively dramatic or MELODRAMATIC; theatrical; overacted

Suppose you are walking on the boardwalk with your boyfriend and he points to your feet and says, "You have Fred Flintstone big toes!" Would you ignore the comment, respond with **MEASURED** (restrained) sarcasm, or throw a **HISTRIONIC** fit? When this happened on MTV's *Jersey Shore*, Sammi "Sweetheart" predictably became **OVERWROUGHT** and **MELODRAMATICALLY** broke up with Ronnie.

381 | PLACATE

To soothe or calm; to appease

In the movie *Clueless*, Cher reacts with great **CONSTERNATION** (Word 368) when she discovers that Mr. Hall has given her a C in debate. Cher skillfully **PLACATES** her concerned father by claiming that "some teachers are trying to low-ball me." As the daughter of a high-powered lawyer, Cher views her grades as "a first offer" and promises to use them as "a jumping-off point to start negotiations." **PLACATED** by Cher's strategy, her father agrees to wait. His patience is rewarded when Cher successfully argues her way from a C to an A-.

382 | ESCHEW

To avoid; to shun; to stay clear of

What do the beatniks of the 1950s and the hippies of the 1960s have in common? Both **ESCHEWED** the conventional middle-class lifestyle of their times. The beatniks **ESCHEWED** conformity and materialism. Preferring to pursue a more communal lifestyle, the hippies **ESCHEWED** commercialism and competition.

383 | STOPGAP

A temporary solution designed to meet an urgent need

The Great Depression confronted the United States with an **UNPRE-CEDENTED** (Word 279) economic crisis. In 1933 during the famous Hundred Days, Congress responded by passing a series of emergency bills. Critics promptly attacked the National Industrial Recovery Act (NIRA), the Agricultural Adjustment Act (AAA), and other New Deal programs by calling them **STOPGAP** measures that at best provided only short-term relief. Historians now argue that the New Deal included both long-term reforms such as Social Security and **STOPGAP** programs that **MITIGATED** (Word 31) but did not end the Depression.

384 | FLOTSAM

The floating wreckage of a ship; debris

According to legend, the Kraken was a huge, many-armed creature that could reach as high as the top of a sailing ship's main mast. In *Pirates of the Caribbean: Dead Man's Chest*, the Kraken destroyed the *Black Pearl*, leaving only scattered **FLOTSAM** floating on the ocean surface.

While **FLOTSAM** typically refers to floating wreckage, it can also refer to cosmic debris. For example, the asteroid Eugenia is one of thousands of bits of cosmic **FLOTSAM** in the great asteroid belt between the orbits of the planets Mars and Jupiter.

385 | CHURLISH, SULLEN, SURLY

Ill-tempered; rude; lacking civility

Tip for a Direct Hit

In Anglo-Saxon times a CHURL was the lowest-ranking freeman in the social HIERARCHY (ranking), the opposite of a thane or knight. These RUSTIC (Word 79) peasants eventually gave their label to today's rude, surly, ill-bred CHURLS, who can now come from any walk of life! Another word for the common man that, over time, acquired an insulting connotation is VILLEIN, the most common type of serf in medieval times. The meaning of the VILLAIN as the evil character in a novel or play dates only from 1822. Interestingly, the word SURLY comes from "sirly," which meant lordly, imperious, and SUPERCILIOUS (Word 395). Apparently anyone on the social ladder could behave badly!

Charlie Harper of *Two and A Half Men* was known for his **CHURLISH** personality. Insensitive to others' feelings, he always said whatever came into his mind. Charlie was especially **SURLY** to his mother. Take a look at this excerpt where Charlie compared his mother to *The Grinch Who Stole Christmas*:

Charlie: *What's mom doing here?*

Alan (his brother): *Well, it is Christmas Eve, Charlie.*

Charlie: *I know. Why isn't she out stealing toys in Whoville?*

386 | RESTITUTION

The act of making good or compensating for a loss, damage, or injury

In 1942, the U.S. Army's Western Defense Command ordered the forced evacuation of 110,000 Japanese-Americans living on the Pacific Coast. Fearing that they might act as **SABOTEURS** (subversive agents) for Japan, the government ordered Japanese–Americans to pack up their belongings and move to "relocation centers" hastily erected farther inland. It was not until 46 years later that the U.S. government officially apologized for its action and approved a **RESTITUTION** payment of $20,000 to each camp survivor.

387 | DISQUIETING

Disturbing; upsetting; vexing; causing unease; worrisome

In the movie *A Walk to Remember*, Landon falls in love with Jamie and is transformed from a **CHURLISH** (Word 386) **BOOR** (Word 64) into a sensitive person who is beginning to find himself. But Landon receives a severe jolt when Jamie reveals some very **DISQUIETING** information about her health. She has leukemia and has stopped responding to treatment. Although shocked by Jamie's **DISQUIETING** story, Landon's love nonetheless remains steadfast.

388 | ORNATE

Characterized by elaborate and expensive decorations; LAVISH

During the 1930's, 85 million Americans a week watched a movie at their local movie palace. The **ORNATE** movie palaces boasted **LAVISH** decorations and elaborate lobbies where people could escape from the hard times of the Great Depression. The "Fabulous Fox" in Atlanta, for example, featured an **ECLECTIC** (Word 391) blend of Asian decorative motifs, the second-largest theater organ in the world, and luxurious light fixtures and furniture. Today, enormous multiplexes have **SUPPLANTED** (replaced) the old **ORNATE** movie palaces. Interestingly, a grass-roots campaign led by local high school students saved the Fox. Today, the **ORNATE** building is a National Historic Landmark and a successful multi-purpose performing arts center.

389 | EXECRABLE, ODIOUS, REPUGNANT
Detestable; repulsive; extremely bad

Third-hand smoke has an odor which is **ODIOUS**. To be more specific, third-hand smoke is the nicotine residue that is left behind on furniture, walls, and carpeting after a cigarette has been smoked in a room. These **EXECRABLE** particles are so small that they can penetrate the deepest portion of the lung, a **REPUGNANT** result, especially for young children. Third-hand smoke is a recently discovered risk of smoking. Research to determine the exact magnitude of the negative health implications is ongoing.

KNOW YOUR ROOTS		
LATIN ROOT:	PUGNACIOUS	disposed to fight, quarrelsome, combative
PUGN, fighting (from	PUGILIST	a boxer, one who fights with his fists
PUG *pugnus*, a fist)	IMPUGN	to fight against, attack, challenge the motives of

390 | PERSPICACIOUS, PRESCIENT, DISCERNING
Insightful, perceptive

What do the French political writer Alexis de Tocqueville and the Jedi Master Yoda have in common? Both were unusually **PERSPICACIOUS**. De Tocqueville visited the United States in 1831 and published his observations four years later. De Tocqueville **PRESCIENTLY** predicted that the debate over slavery would tear the Union apart and that the United States and Russia were destined to be rivals. Like de Tocqueville, Yoda was also an unusually **DISCERNING** observer of human nature. For example, Yoda was **PERSPICACIOUS** when he realized that the young Anakin Skywalker could be seduced by the dark side of the Force. Yoda's **PRESCIENT** insight proved true when Anakin became the villainous Darth Vader.

KNOW YOUR ROOTS

LATIN ROOT:			
SPIC, **SPECT**	look, watch, see, observe	CONSPICUOUS	open to view, attracting attention, obvious, prominent, remarkable
		INSPECT	to look at carefully, to examine critically or officially
		INTROSPECTION	looking into one's own mind, observation and analysis of oneself
		RETROSPECT	looking back on the past
		SPECTACLE	a sight, a show, a pageant, an eyeglass
		SPECULATE	to look at different aspects, to meditate, to theorize, to take part in risky business ventures
		SPECIMEN	that by which a thing is seen and recognized (literally), a sample or one individual of a group
		PROSPECT	view, scene, something hoped for, chance for success
		ASPECT	appearance to the eye, a feature

---

391 | ECLECTIC

Choosing or using a variety of sources

A person with **ECLECTIC** taste in music would like Beethoven, Akon, Linkin Park, Rihanna, Carrie Underwood, and Justin Bieber. Similarly, a teacher with an **ECLECTIC** repertoire of lesson strategies might play YouTube videos, assign internet projects, allow students to hold debates using Twitter, and give lectures.

392 | HIATUS

An interruption in time or continuity; a break

During the 1980s, Harrison Ford starred in three hugely successful movies featuring the adventures of Indiana Jones. After a 19-year **HIATUS**, Indy finally returned as the world's best-known archaeologist in *Indiana Jones and the Kingdom of the Crystal Skull*. Interestingly, executive producer George Lucas and director Steven Spielberg set *Crystal Skull* in 1957, exactly 19 years after the events in *Indiana Jones and the Last Crusade*. Thus, the **HIATUS** in the movies paralleled the **HIATUS** in the real world.

393 | VERTIGINOUS

*Characterized by or suffering from dizziness; having **VERTIGO***

What do the films *Blair Witch Project* and *Cloverfield* have in common? Although fictional, both films were presented as documentaries pieced together from amateurish footage. As a result, both films left many movie goers feeling **VERTIGINOUS**. This **VERTIGINOUS** effect was particularly pronounced in *Cloverfield*. Shot and edited to look as if filmed with a hand-held camera, *Cloverfield* included numerous jump-cuts that created a sense of **VERTIGO**, especially among those who sat near the screen.

394 | ESOTERIC, ARCANE

*Characterized by knowledge that is known only to a small group of specialists; obscure; **RECONDITE***

Have you ever heard of the Resolute Desk located in the Oval Office of the White House? Most people know little or nothing about the desk. Benjamin Franklin Gates in the movies *National Treasure* and *National Treasure: Book of Secrets*, a storehouse of **ESOTERIC** information. Gates demonstrates his knowledge of **ARCANE** facts by explaining that the Resolute Desk was made of wood from the British warship HMS Resolute and then given to President Hayes by Queen Victoria. Gates further demonstrates his knowledge of **RECONDITE** details when he explains that FDR placed a panel in front of the desk to prevent visitors from seeing his leg braces.

395 | SUPERCILIOUS

Showing haughty disdain or arrogant superiority

On *Gossip Girl*, Leighton Meester plays the spoiled, devious, and **SUPERCILIOUS** princess Blair Waldorf. Ironically, as a teenager Leighton had to endure the haughty stares of **SUPERCILIOUS** classmates at Beverly Hills High School. The **SUPERCILIOUS** real-life 90210 students made fun of Leighton because she didn't wear designer clothes or drive an expensive car. "I wasn't very trendy," Leighton now admits. "I didn't wear makeup, and I dressed in jeans and T-shirts."

396 | BLITHE

Joyous; sprightly; mirthful; light; vivacious

The Romantic poet Percy Shelley wrote a poem called "To a Skylark" which begins "Hail to thee, blithe Spirit!/Bird thou never wert" and which celebrates the freedom and joyous, carefree life of the soaring skylark. In the poem Shelley likens himself, the poet, to the bird.

The British playwright Noel Coward wrote a comedy called *Blithe Spirit*, first staged in 1941 and often revived since, in which the phrase is used somewhat **IRONICALLY** (Word 226). A novelist has a **CLAIRVOYANT** (Word 115) conduct a séance which summons up the spirit of his dead first wife, who **BLITHELY** proceeds to wreak havoc with his current marriage. Eventually the second wife dies, and both wives return as spirits to cause more chaos in his life.

397 | UNDERWRITE

To assume financial responsibility for

The Bill and Melinda Gates Foundation is the largest charitable foundation in the world. Its endowment of $38.7 billion enables the foundation to **UNDERWRITE** numerous projects in the United States and around the world. For example, the Gates Millennium Scholars Fund **UNDERWRITES** a $1 billion program to provide scholarships for outstanding minority students.

398 | DISCOMFITED

Uneasy; in a state of embarrassment

In the movie *Princess Diaries*, Mia is a shy tenth-grade student who attends a private school in San Francisco. Mia is shocked when she discovers that she is heir to the throne of Genovia, a small European principality ruled by her grandmother, Queen Clarisse. Persuaded to attend "princess lessons," Mia feels **DISCOMFITED** as she learns the etiquette of being a princess. Mia's feelings of **DISCOMFITURE** are **EXACERBATED** (Word 271) when she attends her school's annual beach party and is embarrassed when Josh deliberately kisses her in front of a group of photographers and when Lana helps photographers take pictures of her clad only in a towel.

399 | TACITURN

Habitually quiet; uncommunicative

Have you watched the movies *Clerks, Clerks II, Chasing Amy, Mall Rats,* or *Jay and Silent Bob Strike Back*? All of these movies feature a character named Silent Bob. Silent Bob smokes too much, often wears a long coat and a backward baseball cap, and as his nickname suggests, seldom talks. He is thus **TACITURN**. Silent Bob usually relies on hand gestures and facial expressions to communicate his feelings. Although normally **TACITURN**, Silent Bob offers **ASTUTE** (perceptive, shrewd) observations on the few occasions when he does speak.

400 | SINECURE

An office or position that provides an income for little or no work

Tip for a Direct Hit

The noun *sinecure* comes from the Latin *sine cura*, meaning "without care." Originally it described a paid church position that did not include caring for the souls of parishioners. That work was delegated to the parish assistant or "curate." A related word is CURATOR, a person who cares for a museum or art collection.

Today it is more typical for a **SINECURE** to be a payback for political contributions or for a family member who needs employment.

In the movie *Batman Begins*, Bruce Wayne is a billionaire businessman who lives in Gotham City. To the world at large, Wayne holds a **SINECURE** at Wayne Enterprises that enables him to act as an irresponsible, **SUPERFICIAL** playboy (see Word 90) who lives off his family's personal fortune. Of course, this **SINECURE** and the Bruce Wayne persona are masks that enable Wayne to hide his secret identity as the Caped Crusader, Batman.

401 | COSMOPOLITAN

Worldly; sophisticated; open-minded and aware of the big picture

PROVINCIAL, PAROCHIAL, INSULAR

Limited in perspective; narrow; restricted in scope and outlook

Tip for a Direct Hit

The contrast between COSMOPOLITAN and PROVINCIAL outlooks can be traced back to their origins. COSMOPOLITAN is derived from the Greek words *kosmos* or "world" and *polites* or "citizen." So a COSMOPOLITAN person is literally a citizen of the world. In contrast, a province is an outlying part of an empire or nation, so a PROVINCIAL person would have a more limited perspective. PAROCHIAL and INSULAR are synonyms that refer to a narrow outlook. PAROCHIAL is derived from parish, a small administrative unit with just one pastor, and INSULAR is derived from the Latin word *insula* meaning "island."

Pretend that you are the editor of a newspaper serving a community of 75,000 people. A local middle school teacher has just been named the city's "teacher of the year." At the same time, a story has just come into your office describing changing admission standards in the nation's top universities and colleges. Which story would you place on your paper's front page? Your decision will probably depend upon whether you have a **COSMOPOLITAN** or a **PROVINCIAL** outlook. A **COSMOPOLITAN** editor would favor a "big picture" outlook and give precedence to the national story. A **PROVINCIAL** editor would favor the local story.

402 | LUGUBRIOUS

Sad, mournful, MELANCHOLIC

While **LUGUBRIOUS** is frequently used to describe sad, mournful music, it can also be used to describe **MELANCHOLY** people. *USA Today* describes the **LUGUBRIOUS** "love hurts" connection between Bella and Edward in *The Twilight Saga: New Moon*, and *Boxoffice Magazine* writes about *The Twilight Saga: Breaking Dawn Part I* "among happy samba-ing Brazilians, Edward and Bella slow-dance just like at their wedding: the world's most **LUGUBRIOUS** couple never speeds up the tempo. The most memorable part of their wedding is their making out at the altar for a good 30 seconds."

In *Star Wars: Episode III Revenge of the Sith*, Padme's death and funeral are accompanied by a **LUGUBRIOUS** musical score. Similarly, in *Titanic* the musicians play a **LUGUBRIOUS** hymn as the great but doomed ship slowly sinks into the Atlantic Ocean.

403 | FECUND

Intellectually productive or inventive, fertile

What do George Lucas and J.K. Rowling have in common? Both have unusually **FECUND** imaginations. In his Star Wars **SAGA** (Word 231), George Lucas created an intergalactic empire populated by humans, alien creatures, robotic droids, Jedi Knights, and Sith Lords. J.K. Rowling's fertile imagination created a secret magical world populated by wizards, witches, dragons, goblins, giants, and elves.

404 | OSTENTATIOUS

Showy; intended to attract notice; pretentious

Wearing **OSTENTATIOUS** jewelry has a long history. Egyptian pharaohs, European rulers, and Mughal sultans all enjoyed wearing **OSTENTATIOUS** jewelry. For example, Queen Elizabeth I's wardrobe included 2,000 **RESPLENDENT** (dazzling) jewel-covered gowns and a diamond-covered tiara.

The passion for wearing **OSTENTATIOUS** jewelry has not gone out of fashion. Commonly referred to as "bling," **OSTENTATIOUS** jewelry is a hallmark of hip-hop culture. For example, Rick Ross, well known for his **OSTENTATIOUS** jewelry, purchased a chain featuring a pendant with an image of himself. The eye-catching piece includes Big Boss's trademark shades and reportedly cost $200,000.

405 | GUILE

Treacherous cunning; skillful deceit

What do Supreme Chancellor Palpatine (*Star Wars Episode III: Revenge of the Sith*), King Edward I (*Braveheart*), and Cher (*Clueless*) all have in common? They all use **GUILE** to achieve their goals. Supreme Chancellor Palpatine uses **GUILE** to deceive Anakin, King Edward I uses **GUILE** to capture William Wallace, and Cher uses **GUILE** to trick Mr. Hall into falling in love with Ms. Guise so that he will be blissfully happy and thus raise everyone's grades.

406 | SANGUINE
Cheerfully confident; optimistic

NASA's Space Transportation System, the United States government's official vehicle launch program, began in 1981. The program sponsored 135 flights over a total of more than 1300 days. The final launch of the shuttle program took place on July 8, 2011, as the program was **CURTAILED** (Word 98) by cost-cutting mandates. However, NASA administrator Charles Bolden is still **SANGUINE**, believing there is still a future for Americans in space using other vehicles and methods:

"As a former astronaut and the current NASA Administrator," he said, "I'm here to tell you that American leadership in space will continue for at least the next half-century because we have laid the foundation for success—and failure is not an option."

407 | SCINTILLATING
Sparkling; shining; brilliantly clever

If you want to attend the University of Chicago, you need a **SCINTILLATING**, creative imagination. The University of Chicago's supplemental application is renowned for its **PROVOCATIVE** (Word 82) essay prompts, which are submitted to the admissions office by current freshmen at the university. The admissions committee uses these prompts to encourage students to develop **SCINTILLATING** responses, in contrast to the **HACKNEYED** (Word 36) products that many admissions committees read about mission trips, community service projects, or family trips "that changed my life." Take a look at these recent essay prompts:

- What does Play-Doh™ have to do with Plato?
- Don't write about reverse psychology.
- How do you feel about Wednesday?

408 | PRISTINE
Remaining in a pure state; uncorrupted by civilization

Sandwiched between Latin American giants Venezuela and Brazil, Guyana is a small country with a vital global asset. About 80 percent of the country is covered by a **PRISTINE** rainforest called the Guyana Shield. The Shield is one of only four intact **PRISTINE** rainforests left on the planet. It is home to 1,400 vertebrate species, 1,680 bird species, and some of the world's most-endangered species, including the jaguar, anaconda, and giant anteater. In a ground-breaking agreement, the government of Guyana announced that in return for development aid, it will place over one million acres of **PRISTINE** rainforest under the protection of a British-led international body.

409 | RAMPANT
Unrestrained; unchecked

While Guyana is taking steps to protect its rainforest, the once **PRISTINE** (Word 408) Amazon rainforest is being dramatically reduced by **RAMPANT** development led by cattle ranchers and loggers. Unless this **RAMPANT** deforestation is **ARRESTED** (Word 281), the Amazon rainforest will be reduced by 40 percent in the next 20 years, resulting in the irreversible loss of thousands of species of plants and animals.

410 | PERNICIOUS
Highly injurious; destructive; deadly

Francisco Santos, the Vice-President of Columbia, launched an international campaign to warn people about the **PERNICIOUS** consequences of cocaine trafficking. Santos made an example of Kate Moss, the British supermodel photographed allegedly snorting cocaine. "When she snorted a line of cocaine, she put land mines in Columbia, she killed people in Columbia, she displaced people in Columbia," Santos told a concerned audience. The **PERNICIOUS** consequences of cocaine trafficking also extend to the environment. "She destroyed the environment," Santos continued. "We have lost two million hectares (about five million acres) of **PRISTINE** (Word 408) rainforest to drug trafficking."

411 | OBLIVIOUS

Lacking conscious awareness; unmindful; unaware

A Staten Island teenager learned the meaning of **OBLIVIOUS** and **MALODOROUS** (Word 199) the hard way. While walking down a neighborhood street, she was so busy texting that she failed to notice an open manhole in front of her. The **OBLIVIOUS** high schooler suddenly fell five feet into a pool of **MALODOROUS** sewage. Fortunately, she only suffered a few minor cuts and bruises. Her accident is a **MALODOROUS** reminder that you should not be **OBLIVIOUS** to your surroundings as you focus on texting messages.

412 | REFRACTORY

OBSTINATELY (Word 15) resistant to authority or control

Do you believe that it is possible to create a utopian community? From the Puritan communities at Massachusetts Bay to the hippie communes in the 1960s, many people have tried and failed to create utopias. While there are many reasons why utopian communities have failed, the sheer **REFRACTORINESS** of human nature is a leading cause. Petty quarrels and jealous disputes provide all-too-common examples of **REFRACTORY** behavior that often undermines even the most idealistic group goals.

413 | GARRULOUS, VERBOSE, LOQUACIOUS
Annoyingly talkative; VOLUBLE

What do Donkey in all the *Shrek* movies and Seth in *Superbad* have in common? Both are very **GARRULOUS**. Donkey often exasperates Shrek with his **VERBOSE** chatter. And Seth is so **LOQUACIOUS** that it is difficult to think of a time when he isn't talking.

414 | CONVIVIAL
Sociable; fond of feasting, drinking, and good company

What do the Deltas in *Animal House* and Ben and his friends in *Knocked Up* have in common? They are all **CONVIVIAL** slackers who love to eat, drink, and party. In fact, Ben and his **CONVIVIAL** buddies are really only **NUANCED** (Word 354) older versions of Bluto and his **CONVIVIAL** fraternity brothers.

415 | BRUSQUE, CURT
Abrupt in manner or speech; discourteously blunt

What do Donald Trump, Dr. House, and Montgomery bus driver J.F. Blake have in common? All three share the trait of being **BRUSQUE**. In the reality show *The Apprentice*, Donald Trump is **BRUSQUE** when he tells each week's losing apprentice, "You're fired!" Dr. House (*House M.D.*) is a medical genius who is very impatient and **CURT** with young doctors who misdiagnose an illness. And finally, J.F. Blake **PRECIPITATED** (Word 283) the Montgomery Bus Boycott when he **CURTLY** ordered Rosa Parks to give up her seat.

416 | TEPID
Lukewarm; mild; half-hearted

The word **TEPID** originated in the Roman baths. Bathers soaked in the hot waters of the *caldarium*, took a cool dip in the *frigidarium*, and finished their day with a refreshing bath in the lukewarm waters of the *tepidarium*. **TEPID** still retains its meaning of being lukewarm or mild. It is most often used when describing lukewarm enthusiasm or praise. For example, Sony was hoping for a hit product in the highly competitive tablet computer market, but its tablets received a **TEPID** response from gadget reviewers and analysts. One analyst stated, "Consumers want tablets, but they are not prepared to pay the same amount they'd pay for an iPad for something that's not an iPad."

Analysts and critics can be wrong. When Apple unveiled the iPhone 4s, it also received a **TEPID** response from technology analysts critiquing its "modest" upgrade. When the hands-on reviews came in, they were very positive, and AT&T reported the biggest first-day sales in its history. One reviewer commented, "I have seen this type of **HUBRIS** (excessive confidence) before from analysts. Some people just want to see Apple fail."

417 | PROTEAN

Readily taking on varied forms and meanings

In Greek mythology Proteus was a sea-god who had two unique abilities. First, he was an **ORACLE** (Word 124) who could foretell the future. Second, he could change his shape to avoid being captured and forced to make predictions. Proteus still lives in the SAT word **PROTEAN**. Test writers often use **PROTEAN** in difficult sentence completion questions about viruses that are hard to target because of their ability to mutate. For example, the HIV virus has proven to be particularly difficult to treat because of its **PROTEAN** nature.

418 | SOLICITOUS

Showing great care and concern; attentive

In *Harry Potter and the Sorcerer's Stone*, Vernon and Petunia Dursley grudgingly raise Harry, depriving him of love and attention. In contrast, they are very **SOLICITOUS** of their only child, Dudley. While they force Harry to sleep in a tiny closet beneath the staircase, Vernon and Petunia give the spoiled Dudley everything he wants. For example, when an irate Dudley complains that he only received 37 birthday presents, one fewer than the year before, his excessively **SOLICITOUS** parents promise to buy him two more gifts.

419 | DISINGENUOUS
INSINCERE; NOT straightforward; NOT CANDID;

What do the leaders of North Korea and Iran have in common? Both have been **DISINGENUOUS** about the true purpose of their nuclear programs. For years, the North Koreans **DISINGENUOUSLY** insisted their nuclear program was designed for peaceful purposes. However, in 2009, North Korea tested an atomic weapon and announced that they were now "a full-fledged nuclear power." Iranian leaders have also insisted their nuclear program is totally peaceful. Critics contend that the Iranians are being **DISINGENUOUS** and that their true goal is to develop weapons of mass destruction.

420 | VENERATE, REVERE
To regard with great respect; to hold in high esteem

What do George Washington and Nelson Mandela have in common? Both men are **VENERATED** as statesmen who played indispensable roles in the history of their countries. As **EULOGIZED** (Word 234) in 1799 by General Henry "Lighthouse Harry" Lee, George Washington is **REVERED** as a leader who was "First in war, first in peace, and first in the hearts of his countrymen." Nelson Mandela is **VENERATED** for his long struggle against apartheid and his leadership in helping South Africa become a multi-racial democracy.

421 | CONTENTIOUS

Quarrelsome; argumentative; likely to provoke a controversy;
DISPUTATIOUS

Many film critics rank Mel Gibson's *The Passion of the Christ* as the most controversial movie ever made. The film provoked **CONTENTIOUS** arguments between supporters, who praised its unflinching depiction of Christ's suffering, and critics, who denounced Gibson's biblical interpretations. These **CONTENTIOUS** arguments provoked a firestorm of publicity that helped the film gross $370 million.

422 | PRECLUDE

To make impossible; to rule out; to prevent

In *Harry Potter and the Sorcerer's Stone*, Harry learns that he is a wizard with a tragic past and a prophesied future. Harry's status as "the Chosen One" who must ultimately confront Lord Voldemort **PRECLUDES** his having a normal life. As a living legend in the wizard world, Harry is recognized wherever he goes. Unlike Superman and Batman, he cannot avoid unwanted attention by adopting a secret persona. With anonymity **PRECLUDED**, he must publicly fulfill his destiny.

423 | COMPUNCTION, CONTRITION, REMORSE, PENITENCE

Feelings of sincere and deep regret

On June 22, 2009, Chris Brown pleaded guilty to assaulting his former girlfriend Rihanna in a February incident. Four weeks later, the R&B singer issued a video apology, saying, "What I did was inexcusable. I am very sad and very ashamed of what I've done." But was this public statement of **CONTRITION** too little and too late? Opinion polls show that the public is evenly divided between those who believe Brown is truly **REMORSEFUL** and **PENITENT** and those who believe his statement of **COMPUNCTION** is an insincere attempt to revive his faltering career.

424 | DEMOGRAPHY

The study of the characteristics of human populations

Tip for a Direct Hit

DEMOGRAPHY and DEMOGRAPHIC have become popular words on both the SAT and AP tests. For example, AP US History exams often have questions about such DEMOGRAPHIC characteristics as the size and movement of American population groups.

Channels like MTV, The CW, and ABC Family target audiences between the ages of 12 and 34, gearing their programming toward this **DEMOGRAPHIC** group. Many of the programs on these networks, like *Jersey Shore, Gossip Girl,* and *Pretty Little Liars* are the most-watched shows by audiences 12 to 34. Young adults are a **DEMOGRAPHIC** group highly prized by clothing, soft drink, and cosmetic companies. Sponsors carefully study the **DEMOGRAPHIC** characteristics of television viewers as they make multi-million dollar advertising decisions. Many of these companies advertise during the best-rated shows on MTV, The CW, and ABC Family in order to reach the key young adult **DEMOGRAPHIC** group.

425 | APHORISM, AXIOM

A statement universally accepted as true; a MAXIM

Benjamin Franklin's famous *Autobiography* contains a storehouse of wise **APHORISMS**. For example, Franklin earnestly warned students that "by failing to prepare, you are preparing to fail." Franklin's **AXIOM** is still valid. Let us **EXHORT** (Word 53) you to study the words in your *Direct Hits* vocabulary books. Always remember this three-word **AXIOM**: "Vocabulary! Vocabulary! Vocabulary!"

426 | JUXTAPOSE

To place side by side or in close PROXIMITY (nearness)

JUXTAPOSITION

The position of being close together or side by side

A remix is an alternative version of a song, often created by a **JUXTAPOSITION** of new lyrics over the same rhythm, or vice versa.

The Grey Album is a famous mix-tape produced by Danger Mouse that features 12 remixed songs. Each song **JUXTAPOSES** the lyrics of Jay-Z's *The Black Album* with instrumentals from the Beatles' *White Album*.

427 | BOMBASTIC

POMPOUS (Word 94) or PRETENTIOUS in speech or writing; OSTENTATIOUSLY (Word 404) lofty in style

Tip for a Direct Hit

BOMBAST comes from the Latin *bombax* meaning "cotton" and Greek *bombyx*, "silkworm or garment of silk," and in its original concrete usage referred to a form of stuffing made from cotton, wool, horsehair, or other loose material used to pad and shape garments—the shoulders, chest, stomach, sleeves, and even men's hose. Though never seen in public, this stuffing was essential to men's and women's clothing in the 16th century. Today the word BOMBAST is used more abstractly to describe another kind of padding—in speech or writing. This padded, inflated style can be described as GRANDILOQUENT (literally, speaking grandly) and BOMBASTIC.

Sheldon and Leonard portray hyper-intelligent and ultra-nerdy physicists on the hit sitcom *The Big Bang Theory*. While Leonard tries very hard to convince people he is not a nerd, Sheldon believes himself a super-genius, and he is very vocal in describing his intelligence. He frequently belittles his peers with his **PRETENTIOUS** (putting on an appearance of importance) speech. Sheldon's **BOMBASTIC** ego is a source of great humor on the show. Here is the dialogue he and Leonard have when they meet their new charming next-door neighbor, Penny.

Leonard: *So, tell us about you.*

Penny: *Um, me? Okay—I'm a Sagittarius, which probably tells you way more than you need to know.*

Sheldon: *Yes—it tells us that you participate in the mass cultural delusion that the sun's apparent position relative to arbitrarily defined constellations at the time of your birth somehow affects your personality.*

Penny: [stares at Sheldon in utter confusion] *Participateinthewhat?*

Leonard: [scrambling to save face] *I think what Sheldon is trying to say is that Sagittarius wouldn't have been our first guess.*

Penny: *Oh.*

428 | FORBEARANCE

Abstaining from the enforcement of a right; the act of refraining from acting on a desire or impulse

You might be interested in knowing about **FORBEARANCE** if you take out student loans to pay for college. If you face financial difficulty after graduating, then **FORBEARANCE** can save you from defaulting on the loan. **FORBEARANCE** by the lender allows you to suspend your student loan payments for a period of time, often a year.

On *The King of Queens*, Doug Heffernan's **IRASCIBLE** (quick to anger) father-in-law, Arthur Spoon lives in Doug's basement. Arthur **PROVOKES** (Word 82) the usually **AMIABLE** (Word 18) Doug with his antics, such as stealing money from Doug's nightstand and screaming to embarrass him in public. Though Doug is the head of his household and has good reasons to kick Arthur out, he exhibits **FORBEARANCE** to please his wife, Carrie.

429 | UNFETTERED

Freed from restraint of any kind; liberated

There is an on-going debate in education over whether students should have **UNFETTERED** access to the Internet through school computers and libraries. Most schools have "Acceptable Use" policies to provide students and teachers with the most wide-ranging educational experiences possible, while still protecting them from **PERNICIOUS** (Word 410) materials or sites. The procedures do not attempt to articulate all allowable or all **PROSCRIBED** (Word 430) behavior by users., leaving users ultimately responsible for their actions in accessing and using school computers and networks.

Lewis Carroll, J.K. Rowling, and JRR Tolkien have all used their **UNFETTERED** imaginations to create fantasy worlds that have blurred the boundaries between adult and children's literature.. All three have also had their works transformed into blockbuster movies.

430 | PRESCRIBE

To require; to order; to direct

PROSCRIBE

To forbid; to prohibit; to outlaw

Even though **PRESCRIBE** and **PROSCRIBE** sound similar, be careful, because the two verbs are virtual opposites. The confusion comes from the prefix *pro*, which usually means "for" or "favoring" but in this case means "in front of." In ancient Rome **PROSCRIBE** meant "to publish the name of a person condemned to death or banishment." Now it has come to mean "to prohibit."

During the Prohibition Era (1919 to 1933) the manufacture, sale, or transportation of alcohol was **PROSCRIBED** in the U.S. Now alcohol consumption by adults is permitted, but each state may **PRESCRIBE** its minimum drinking age. In 1984 President Ronald Reagan responded to the tragic **ANECDOTES** (Word 233) told by Mothers Against Drunk Driving (MADD) of accidents involving young people driving to states with lower drinking ages. The National Minimum Drinking Age Act pressured the states to **PROSCRIBE** the purchase and possession of alcohol by anyone under the age of 21 or lose ten percent of their annual federal highway apportionment.

The College Board also **PROSCRIBES** the use of cell phones in the testing room. We would **PRESCRIBE** taking a watch (with the alarm off) to the test so that you can stay **COGNIZANT** (aware) of your time on each section.

FAST REVIEW

Quick Definitions

Volume 2 contains 210 words, each of which is illustrated with vivid pop culture, historic, and literary examples. The Fast Review is designed to provide you with an easy and efficient way to review each of these words. We recommend that you put a check beside each word that you know. That way you can quickly identify the words you are having trouble remembering. Focus on each hard-to-remember word by going over its definition, reviewing its examples, and trying to come up with your own memory tip.

Good luck with your review. Don't expect to learn all of these words at once. Frequent repetition is the best way to learn and remember new words.

CHAPTER 7: RHETORICAL/LITERARY TERMS

221. **FIGURATIVE/METAPHORICAL LANGUAGE**—A general term referring to language that describes a thing in terms of something else. The resemblance is FIGURATIVE, not LITERAL, as the reader is carried beyond the LITERAL meaning to consider the NUANCES and connotations of the words used in the comparison.

222. **SIMILE**—An EXPLICIT figure of speech that is a comparison between two essentially unlike things, usually using the words "like" or "as," which points out a FIGURATIVE way that the two things ARE alike.

223. **METAPHOR**—In its more narrow sense, a figure of speech in which one thing is described in terms of another using an IMPLICIT or implied comparison, without the use of "like" or "as."

224. **PERSONIFICATION**—A figure of speech in which an inanimate object is given human qualities or abilities

225. **PARALLELISM/PARALLEL STRUCTURE**—A rhetorical device or SYNTACTICAL construction which involves using matching grammatical patterns to establish the equivalent relationship or importance of two or more items. PARALLELISM provides balance and authority to sentences.

226. **IRONY**—A figure of speech in which what we say or write conveys the opposite of its literal meaning

227. **SYNOPSIS**—A brief summary of the major points of a thesis, theory, story or literary work; an abstract; a PRÉCIS

228. **SATIRE, LAMPOON, PARODY**—A work that ridicules human vices and follies; comic criticism. Note that LAMPOON and PARODY are often used as verbs meaning to ridicule.

229. **HYPERBOLE**—A figure of speech in which exaggeration is used for emphasis or effect; extreme exaggeration

230. **CARICATURE**—A representation in which the subject's distinctive features or peculiarities are deliberately exaggerated for comic effect

231. **EPIC**—A long narrative poem written in a grand style to celebrate the feats of a legendary hero
SAGA—A long narrative story; a heroic tale

232. **FORESHADOWING**—A suggestion or indication that something will

happen in a story; a hint that PRESAGES

233. **ANECDOTE**—A short account of an interesting or humorous incident

234. **EULOGY**—A LAUDATORY speech or written tribute, especially one praising someone who has died

235. **ALLUSION**—An indirect or brief reference to a person, event, place, phrase, piece of art, or literary work that assumes a common knowledge with the reader or listener

CHAPTER 8: SCIENCE AND THE SOCIAL SCIENCES

236. **CATALYST**—In chemistry, a CATALYST is a substance (such as an enzyme) that accelerates the rate of a chemical reaction at some temperature, but without itself being transformed or consumed by the reaction. In everyday usage a CATALYST is any agent that provokes or triggers change.

237. **CAUSTIC**—In chemistry, a CAUSTIC substance is one that burns or destroys organic tissue by chemical action. Hydrofluoric acid and silver nitrate are examples of CAUSTIC substances. In everyday usage, a CAUSTIC comment is one that hurts or burns.

238. **CRYSTALLIZE**—In chemistry, CRYSTALLIZATION is the process by which crystals are formed. In everyday usage, to CRYSTALLIZE means to give a definite form to an idea or plan.

239. **OSMOSIS**—In chemistry, OSMOSIS refers to the diffusion of a fluid through a semi-permeable membrane until there is an equal concentration of fluid on both sides of the membrane. In everyday usage, OSMOSIS refers to a gradual, often unconscious process of assimilation.

240. **SEDENTARY**—In ecology, animals that are SEDENTARY remain or live in one area. In everyday usage, SEDENTARY means settled and therefore accustomed to sitting or doing little exercise.

241. **VIRULENT**—In medical science, VIRULENT refers to a disease or toxin that is extremely infectious, malignant, or poisonous. In everyday usage, VIRULENT refers to language that is bitterly hostile, hateful, and antagonistic.

242. **EMPIRICAL**—In science, EMPIRICAL means originating in or based on

direct observation and experience. EMPIRICAL data can then be used to support or reject a hypothesis. In everyday language, EMPIRICAL means to be guided by practical experience, not theory.

243. **ENTOMOLOGY**—The scientific study of insects

244. **GESTATE**—In science, GESTATE means to carry within the uterus from conception to delivery. In everyday language, GESTATE means to conceive and develop in the mind.

245. **PARADIGM**—In science, a PARADIGM is a framework or model of thought

246. **ENTREPRENEUR**—A person who organizes and manages a business or enterprise

247. **LUCRATIVE**—Very profitable

248. **EXTRAVAGANT**—Excessive and therefore lacking restraint

249. **AVARICE, CUPIDITY**—Excessive desire for material wealth; greed; COVETOUSNESS

250. **GLUT, PLETHORA, SURFEIT**—A surplus or excess of something

251. **DESTITUTE, IMPOVERISHED, INDIGENT**—Very poor, lacking basic resources
    AFFLUENT, OPULENT—Very rich, having abundant resources

252. **MUNIFICENT**—Very generous

253. **PARSIMONIOUS**—Excessively cheap with money; stingy

254. **DEPRECIATION**—Any decrease or loss in value caused by age, wear, or market conditions

255. **REMUNERATE**—To compensate; to make payment for; to pay a person

256. **ACCORD**—A formal concurrence, agreement, or harmony of minds

257. **ENLIGHTEN, EDIFY**—To inform, instruct, illuminate, and thus remove darkness and ignorance

258. **APPEASEMENT**—The policy of granting concessions to maintain peace

259. **NULLIFY**—To make null; declare invalid

260. **TRIUMVIRATE**—A group or association of three leaders

261. **PRETEXT**—An excuse; an alleged cause

262. **WATERSHED**—Critical point that marks a change of course; a turning point

263. **CONSENSUS**—A general agreement

264. **AUTOCRAT, DESPOT**—A ruler or other person with unlimited power and authority

265. **MANIFESTO**—A public declaration of beliefs, policies, or intentions

266. **ENFRANCHISE**—To endow with the rights of citizenship, especially the right to vote
     DISENFRANCHISE—To deprive of some privilege or right, especially the right to vote

267. **COERCE**—To force to act or think in a certain way by use of pressure, threats, or torture; to compel

268. **EGALITARIAN**—Favoring social equality; believing in a society in which all people have equal political, economic, and civil rights

269. **DEMARCATION**—The setting or marking of boundaries or limits, as a line of demarcation

270. **INQUISITION**—A severe interrogation; a systematic questioning

271. **AMELIORATE**—To make a situation better
     EXACERBATE—To make a situation worse

272. **DESICCATED**—Thoroughly dried out; lifeless, totally arid

273. **CONTIGUOUS**—Sharing an edge or boundary; touching

274. **PERTINENT**—Relevant; to the point; clearly illustrative of a major point

275. **COMPLICITY**—Association or participation in a wrongful act

276. **EXONERATE, EXCULPATE**—To free from guilt or blame

277. **INDISPUTABLE**—Not open to question; undeniable; irrefutable

278. **PRECEDENT**—An act or instance that is used as an example in dealing with subsequent similar instances

279. **UNPRECEDENTED**—Without previous example, never known before; an UNPRECEDENTED event has never happened before

280. **MALFEASANCE**—Misconduct or wrongdoing, especially by a public official

CHAPTER 9: WORDS WITH MULTIPLE MEANINGS

281. **ARREST**—To bring to a stop; halt

282. **GRAVITY**—Seriousness; dignity; solemnity; weight

283. **PRECIPITATE**—To cause, bring about prematurely, hastily or suddenly

284. **RELIEF**—Elevation of a land surface

285. **CHECK**—To restrain; halt; hold back; contain

286. **FLAG**—To become weak, feeble, or spiritless; to lose interest

287. **DISCRIMINATING**—Characterized by the ability to make fine distinctions; having refined taste

288. **ECLIPSE**—Overshadow; outshine; surpass

289. **COIN**—To devise a new word or phrase

290. **STOCK**—A stereotypical and formulaic character in a novel or film

291. **CURRENCY**—General acceptance or use; prevalence

292. **BENT**—A strong tendency; a leaning; an inclination; a PROPENSITY

293. **COURT**—To attempt to gain the favor or support of a person or group; to woo

294. **NEGOTIATE**—To successfully travel through, around, or over an obstacle or terrain

295. **TEMPER**—To soften; to moderate; to MITIGATE

296. **PEDESTRIAN**—Undistinguished; ordinary; conventional

297. **CAVALIER**—Having an arrogant attitude or a haughty disregard for others

298. **SANCTION**—An official approval or disapproval for an action

299. **COMPROMISE**—To reduce the quality or value of something; to jeopardize or place at risk

300. **CHANNEL**—To direct or guide along a desired course

301. **QUALIFY**—To modify; to limit by adding exceptions or restricting conditions

302. **PERSONIFICATION**—A perfect example; embodiment; EPITOME; PARAGON

CHAPTER 10: THE TOUGHEST WORDS I

303. **LAMBASTE**—Denounce; strongly criticize

304. **QUIESCENT**—Marked by inactivity; in a state of quiet repose

305. **PROVISIONAL**—Tentative; temporary; for the time being (like a PROVISIONAL driver's license)

306. **LURID**—Sensational; shocking; ghastly

307. **TRUCULENT, PUGNACIOUS, BELLIGERENT**—Defiantly aggressive; eager to fight

308. **PROPITIATE**—To appease; to conciliate; to regain the favor or goodwill of

309. **ÉLAN**—A vigorous spirit; great enthusiasm

310. **PERFUNCTORY**—Something performed in a spiritless, mechanical, and routine manner

311. **APLOMB**—Self-assurance; confident composure; admirable poise under pressure

312. **OPAQUE**—Hard to understand; impenetrably dense and obscure

313. **CRAVEN**—Cowardly; CONTEMPTIBLY faint-hearted

314. **VENAL**—Corrupt; dishonest; open to bribery

315. **LICENTIOUS**—Immoral; DISSOLUTE; debauched

316. **NOXIOUS**—Harmful; injurious to physical, mental, or moral health

317. **SUPERFLUOUS, EXTRANEOUS**—Unnecessary; extra

318. **DUPLICITOUS**—Deliberately deceptive in behavior or speech

319. **PROFLIGATE**—Wasteful; SQUANDERING time and money by living for the moment

320. **EPIPHANY**—A sudden realization; an insightful moment

321. **INSIDIOUS**—Causing harm in a subtle or stealthy manner; devious

322. **VACUOUS, INANE**—Empty; lacking serious purpose; VAPID

323. **HARBINGER, PORTENT, PRESAGE**—Indications or omens that something important or calamitous is about to occur

324. **BELEAGUER**—To beset; to surround with problems

325. **BURGEON**—To grow rapidly; to expand

326. **IMPERIOUS**—Domineering and arrogant; haughty

327. **PETULANT**—Peevish, irritable

328. **COMPLAISANT**—Agreeable; marked by a pleasing personality;

AFFABLE; AMIABLE

329. **FAWN**—Behaving in a SERVILE, OBSEQUIOUS, or SUBSERVIENT manner

330. **OBDURATE, INTRANSIGENT**—Very stubborn; obstinate; unyieldingly persistent; inflexible; INTRACTABLE

331. **REDOLENT**—Exuding fragrance; full of a specified smell; suggestive of

332. **CHICANERY**—Deception by subterfuge; deliberate trickery

333. **CONUNDRUM**—A difficult problem; a dilemma with no easy solution

334. **SLIGHT**—To treat in a disparaging manner; to deliberately ignore

335. **CAPITULATE**—To surrender; to comply without protest

336. **DISHEARTENING**—Very discouraging; dismaying; dispiriting

337. **APOCRYPHAL**—Of doubtful authenticity; false; SPURIOUS

338. **MAGISTERIAL**—Learned and authoritative

339. **PLASTIC, MALLEABLE, PLIABLE**—Flexible; easily shaped, especially by outside influences or forces

340. **CHAGRIN**—The feeling of distress caused by humiliation, failure, or embarrassment

341. **OBSTREPEROUS**—Noisily and stubbornly defiant; unruly; boisterous

342. **IDYLLIC**—Charmingly simple and carefree

343. **DILAPIDATED**—Having fallen into a state of disrepair; broken-down; in deplorable condition

344. **EXTEMPORIZE, IMPROVISE**—To lecture or speak without notes

345. **MYRIAD**—Many; numerous

346. **UNGAINLY**—Awkward; clumsy; NOT graceful

347. **DILATORY**—Habitually late; tardy

348. **VITUPERATIVE**—Characterized by verbal abuse and bitter criticism

349. **DISCORDANT**—Not in harmony; incompatible; at variance with, as in a DISCORDANT detail that doesn't fit a pattern

350. **PERFIDIOUS**—Treacherous; traitorous; deceitful

351. **PROLIFERATE**—To increase rapidly

352. **INDOMITABLE, RESOLUTE**—Very determined; unwavering

353. **MORIBUND**—Approaching death; about to become OBSOLETE

354. **NUANCE**—A SUBTLE shade of meaning or feeling; a slight degree of difference

355. **FLIPPANT, FACETIOUS**—Treating serious matters with lighthearted humor or lack of respect

356. **CREDULOUS**—Easily convinced; tending to believe too readily; GULLIBLE
INCREDULOUS—Disbelieving, SKEPTICAL

357. **FLORID**—Flowery in style; very ORNATE

358. **EXCORIATING, SCATHING**—Expressing strong disapproval; condemning; loudly DECRYING

359. **INTERLOPER**—An intruder; a gatecrasher

360. **CEREBRAL**—Intellectual rather than emotional
VISCERAL—Instinctive rather than rational

361. **NONPLUSSED, CONFOUNDED**—Utterly PERPLEXED; completely puzzled; totally bewildered

362. **IGNOMINIOUS**—Humiliating; shameful; disgraceful

363. **EUPHONY**—Soothing or pleasant sounds; harmony
CACOPHONY—Harsh, clashing, jarring, grating sounds; disharmony

364. **OBSEQUIOUS**—Promptly obedient, submissive; marked by or exhibiting FAWNING attentiveness

365. **TIMOROUS**—Showing nervousness or fear

CHAPTER 11: THE TOUGHEST WORDS II

366. **IDIOSYNCRASY**—A trait or mannerism that is peculiar to an individual

367. **CENSORIOUS, CAPTIOUS**—Highly critical; fault-finding

368. **CONSTERNATION**—A state of great dismay and confusion

369. **DIDACTIC**—Tending to give instruction or advice; inclined to teach or lecture others too much; containing a political or moral lesson

370. **ELUCIDATE**—To make clear or plain, especially by explanation

371. **EFFUSIVE**—Expressing excessive emotion in an unrestrained manner; gushing

372. **PROLIFIC**—Very productive

373. **FUROR**—A general commotion; an uproar

374. **PARANOIA**—A tendency toward excessive or irrational suspiciousness; irrational fear; delusions of persecution

375. **MARGINAL, PERIPHERAL**—Of secondary importance; NOT central; on the perimeter

376. **OBFUSCATE**—To deliberately confuse; to make something so confusing that it is hard to understand

377. **FLUMMOX**—To confuse; to perplex

378. **SPATE**—A large number or amount

379. **INEFFABLE**—Too overwhelming to be put into words; indescribable; inexpressible

380. **HISTRIONIC, OVERWROUGHT**—Excessively dramatic or MELODRAMATIC; theatrical; overacted

381. **PLACATE**—To soothe or calm; to appease

382. **ESCHEW**—To avoid; to shun; to stay clear of

383. **STOPGAP**—A temporary solution designed to meet an urgent need

384. **FLOTSAM**—The floating wreckage of a ship; debris

385. **CHURLISH, SULLEN, SURLY**—Ill-tempered; rude; lacking civility

386. **RESTITUTION**—The act of making good or compensating for a loss, damage, or injury

387. **DISQUIETING**—Disturbing; upsetting; vexing; causing unease; worrisome

388. **ORNATE**—Characterized by elaborate and expensive decorations; LAVISH

389. **EXECRABLE, ODIOUS, REPUGNANT**—Detestable; repulsive; extremely bad

390. **PERSPICACIOUS, PRESCIENT, DISCERNING**—Insightful, perceptive

391. **ECLECTIC**—Choosing or using a variety of sources

392. **HIATUS**—An interruption in time or continuity; a break

393. **VERTIGINOUS**—Characterized by or suffering from dizziness; having VERTIGO

394. **ESOTERIC, ARCANE**—Characterized by knowledge that is known only to a small group of specialists; obscure; RECONDITE

395. **SUPERCILIOUS**—Showing haughty disdain or arrogant superiority

396. **BLITHE**—Joyous; sprightly; mirthful; light; vivacious

397. **UNDERWRITE**—To assume financial responsibility for

398. **DISCOMFITED**—Uneasy; in a state of embarrassment

399. **TACITURN**—Habitually quiet; uncommunicative

400. **SINECURE**—An office or position that provides an income for little or no work

401. **COSMOPOLITAN**—Worldly; sophisticated; open-minded and aware of the big picture
    PROVINCIAL, PAROCHIAL, INSULAR—Limited in perspective; narrow; restricted in scope and outlook

402. **LUGUBRIOUS**—Sad, mournful, MELANCHOLIC

403. **FECUND**—Intellectually productive or inventive, fertile

404. **OSTENTATIOUS**—Showy; intended to attract notice; pretentious

405. **GUILE**—Treacherous cunning; skillful deceit

406. **SANGUINE**—Cheerfully confident; optimistic

407. **SCINTILLATING**—Sparkling; shining; brilliantly clever

408. **PRISTINE**—Remaining in a pure state; uncorrupted by civilization

409. **RAMPANT**—Unrestrained; unchecked

410. **PERNICIOUS**—Highly injurious; destructive; deadly

411. **OBLIVIOUS**—Lacking conscious awareness; unmindful; unaware

412. **REFRACTORY**—OBSTINATELY resistant to authority or control

413. **GARRULOUS, VERBOSE, LOQUACIOUS**—Annoyingly talkative; VOLUBLE

414. **CONVIVIAL**—Sociable; fond of feasting, drinking, and good company

415. **BRUSQUE, CURT**—Abrupt in manner or speech; discourteously blunt

416. **TEPID**—Lukewarm; mild; half-hearted

417. **PROTEAN**—Readily taking on varied forms and meanings

418. **SOLICITOUS**—Showing great care and concern; attentive

419. **DISINGENUOUS**—INSINCERE; NOT straightforward; NOT CANDID

420. **VENERATE, REVERE**—To regard with great respect; to hold in high esteem

421. **CONTENTIOUS**—Quarrelsome; argumentative; likely to provoke a controversy; DISPUTATIOUS

422. **PRECLUDE**—To make impossible; to rule out; to prevent

423. **COMPUNCTION, CONTRITION, REMORSE, PENITENCE**—Feelings of sincere and deep regret

424. **DEMOGRAPHY**—The study of the characteristics of human populations

425. **APHORISM, AXIOM**—A statement universally accepted as true; a MAXIM

426. **JUXTAPOSE**—To place side by side or in close PROXIMITY
JUXTAPOSITION—The position of being close together or side by side

427. **BOMBASTIC**—POMPOUS or PRETENTIOUS in speech or writing; OSTENTATIOUSLY lofty in style

428. **FORBEARANCE**—Abstaining from the enforcement of a right; the act of refraining from acting on a desire or impulse

429. **UNFETTERED**—Freed from restraint of any kind; liberated

430. **PRESCRIBE**—To require; to order; to direct
PROSCRIBE—To forbid; to prohibit; to outlaw

TESTING YOUR VOCABULARY

Each SAT contains 19 sentence completion questions and 7-8 vocabulary-in-context questions about the reading passages. These vocabulary-based questions determine 30-40% of your critical reading score.

Each sentence completion will always have a key word or phrase that will lead you to the correct answer. The following 35 questions are designed to give you practice using your knowledge of the toughest vocabulary in Volume 2. You'll find the answers and explanations on pages 111–124.

In the movie *300*, director Zach Snyder compares Sparta to a lonely citadel of freedom valiantly holding out against the tyrant Xerxes and his vast horde of Persian soldiers. This heroic image of indomitable Spartans determined to fight to the death remains dominant in popular culture. Without slighting Sparta's contribution to the defense of ancient Greece, it is important to remember that it was the Athenians who sacrificed their city and then defeated the Persian fleet at the watershed battle of Platea.

1. The author suggests that the "lonely citadel of freedom" (line 2) is best understood as

   A an anecdote relaying an important message
   B an unflattering flashback
   C a vivid metaphor for heroic resistance
   D a satirical commentary on Spartan bravery
   E an uninspired simile

Mr. Williams praised Alex's short story for its descriptive vocabulary and impressive use of metaphorical language. However, as an honest and incisive critic, Mr. Williams admonished Alex for failing to explore the relationship between the literal meaning of what his protagonist said and what he really implied.

2. Mr. Williams criticized Alex's short story for its

   A outstanding use of metaphors and similes
   B magisterial tone
   C incoherent structure
   D lack of dramatic irony
   E unrealistic hyperboles

A stunning lack of attention to plot and dialogue are by far the most egregious flaws that plague a movie that should never have been filmed, let alone released.

3. The tone of this sentence is best described as

   A scathing
   B tempered
   C archaic
   D convivial
   E ambiguous

As a dedicated reformer, I.N. Stokes fought against dumbbell tenements, calling them "dirty, overcrowded, degraded places run by exploitive landlords." Stokes' housing reform efforts culminated when, serving on the New York State Tenement House Commission, he co-authored the Tenement House Law of 1901, which required tenements to have a host of new features, including deep backyards, larger rooms, and broad side-courts.

4. I.N. Stokes's attitude toward dumbbell apartments is best described as

   A enlightened advocacy
   B resolute opposition
   C paralyzing ambivalence
   D tempered acquiescence
   E nostalgic reminiscence

At that time, I was a traveling reporter assigned to Frederickson's Senate campaign. As the days turned into weeks, I heard his basic stump speech dozens of times. I soon became bored as Frederickson endlessly repeated clichés and slogans about standing up to the Russians, cutting government waste, and building a new and better America.

5. The author believed that Frederickson's speeches were

   A scintillating
   B divisive
   C truculent
   D supercilious
   E trite

6. The new labor contract was reached by _____ and compromise, not by force and _____ .

   A allusion .. hyperbole
   B malfeasance .. manifesto
   C avarice .. disenfranchisement
   D consensus .. coercion
   E osmosis .. appeasement

7. The forceful personality and generous patronage of Pope Julius II acted as _____ , triggering an outpouring of artistic creativity now known as the High Renaissance.

   A a pretext
   B a metaphor
   C a catalyst
   D an allusion
   E an accord

8. Approved in 1920, the 19th Amendment _____ millions of American women who had been denied the right to vote since the ratification of the Constitution in 1789.

   A enfranchised
   B depreciated
   C remunerated
   D enlightened
   E nullified

9. The mayor's chief of staff successfully cleared herself of charges of _____ by proving that a member of the town council had clandestinely misappropriated the missing funds.

   A belligerence

   B appeasement

   C malfeasance

   D destitution

   E caricature

10. Determined to reduce global carbon dioxide emissions, leading environmentalists called for international _____ to _____ the growth of inefficient coal-burning factories.

    A paradigms .. foster

    B accords .. arrest

    C manifestos .. reaffirm

    D mandates .. encourage

    E anecdotes .. combat

11. The park guide warned the novice hikers to avoid advanced trails that contained rugged natural obstacles and were therefore difficult to _____ .

    A court

    B eclipse

    C nullify

    D enfranchise

    E negotiate

12. Because they were based upon rigorously collected _____ data and not abstract theories, Professor Halle's revolutionary conclusions _____ all previous studies by making them obsolete.

    A experimental .. reinforced

    B stock .. surpassed

    C questionable .. strengthened

    D secondhand .. obliterated

    E empirical .. eclipsed

13. The once upbeat candidate had to _____ her initial optimism as new polling data indicated that her popular support had begun to significantly erode.

    A temper

    B coerce

    C intensify

    D exonerate

    E remunerate

14. Rapper Ludacris' name is actually an amalgam: he combined his given name Chris with the first part of the word ludicrous to _____ his popular stage name.

A check

B court

C precipitate

D coin

E enlighten

15. Americans understood the full _____ of the Cuban Missile Crisis when President Kennedy, calmly but with great seriousness, informed the public that any attack on the United States from Cuba would trigger a full nuclear retaliation against the Soviet Union.

A currency

B extravagance

C virulence

D gravity

E avarice

16. Critics panned the new action adventure film, saying that it was a trite story filled with _____ characters who were both formulaic and stereotypical.

A munificent

B unprecedented

C stock

D anecdotal

E ironic

17. The female subject of this painting by Henri Matisse seems _____ , as if Matisse sought to portray an unconquerable female spirit.

A ungainly

B indomitable

C quiescent

D vacuous

E perfidious

18. Some people alternate between contrasting temperaments; either they are _____ or they are _____ .

A complaisant .. petulant

B indomitable .. resolute

C obdurate .. intractable

D imperious .. domineering

E truculent .. belligerent

19. Daniel Webster's reputation for sublime _____ was reinforced by his learned, authoritative, and even _____ tone when delivering speeches on the Senate floor.

A comedy .. truculent

B diligence .. perfunctory

C oratory .. magisterial

D loyalty .. perfidious

E optimism .. disheartening

20. The salesman was known for both his _____ and his _____ : he lied frequently but did so with great enthusiasm and flair.

A venality .. indifference

B pugnacity .. animation

C petulance .. aloofness

D complicity .. malfeasance

E duplicity .. élan

21. Brianna was a friendly and conciliatory person; she had none of her brother's _____ .

A pugnacity

B affability

C venality

D élan

E extravagance

22. The now disgraced governor was _____ public official, who was corrupt and easily bribed.

A a vituperative

B an obdurate

C a venal

D an imperious

E a craven

23. The American rap artist Lil Wayne is most _____ songwriter of all time, with a record of six #1 hits in one calendar year.

A paranoid

B sanguine

C dilatory

D prolific

E censorious

24. Matthew was both _____ and _____ : he was surly to the point of being rude and arrogant to the point of being obnoxious.

A churlish .. supercilious

B convivial .. imperious

C curt .. histrionic

D verbose .. didactic

E refractory .. sanguine

25. Judy Chicago, an influential contemporary artist, is known for her _____ style, which features an eccentric and highly individualistic interweaving of themes, imagery, and materials.

A pristine

B lugubrious

C idiosyncratic

D apocryphal

E vacuous

26. Parties and other social gatherings benefit from having _____ hosts who provide entertaining company, delicious food, and lively conversation.

A truculent

B refractory

C oblivious

D brusque

E convivial

27. In temperament the two leaders were very different: Janice was convivial, talkative, and at times even _____ ; in contrast, Sherece was unassuming, guarded, and at times even _____ .

A surly .. sullen

B garrulous .. taciturn

C verbose .. effusive

D imperious .. egalitarian

E obstreperous .. censorious

28. Although Caravaggio was a key figure in Rome's emerging new Baroque style of art, he nevertheless perceived himself as being _____ figure with little influence.

A a vital

B a marginal

C an ungainly

D an epic

E a watershed

29. Since many successful composers draw their inspiration from a variety of cultures, styles, and disciplines, their approach could best be called _____ .

A refractory

B vertiginous

C histrionic

D idyllic

E eclectic

30. Art teachers enthusiastically _____ the new clay, saying that its extraordinary _____ enabled students to mold it into almost any shape.

A touted .. buoyancy

B extolled .. plasticity

C expurgated .. eccentricity

D disparaged .. malleability

E reaffirmed .. longevity

31. Theater producers rejected the impenetrably dense screenplay, saying that its _____ rendered it unsuitable for even its most sophisticated and _____ patrons.

A poignancy .. pompous

B superficiality .. clairvoyance

C subtlety .. pragmatic

D opacity .. cosmopolitan

E serendipity .. discerning

32. The governor's emergency measures were intended as _____ , a temporary expedient that called for voluntary water conservation until permanent laws could be put into place.

A a metaphor

B an anecdote

C a conundrum

D an inquisition

E a stopgap

33. Those unfriendly critics who preferred opera that was _____ and melodious found the music of Christopher Markham jarring and warned that his influence on opera would be _____ .

A obstreperous .. lugubrious

B provocative .. platitudinous

C scintillating .. superfluous

D euphonious .. pernicious

E cacophonous .. perfidious

34. Many scientists view the precipitous decline in the populations of both polar bears and penguins as a _____ : an early warning of the deleterious consequences of global warming.

A pretext

B caricature

C portent

D paradigm

E synopsis

35. The late Isaac Asimov was both _____ and _____ : he wrote voluminously while maintaining exacting standards of research.

A didactic .. idiosyncratic

B prolific .. meticulous

C histrionic .. censorious

D discerning .. disquieting

E eclectic .. superficial

ANSWERS AND EXPLANATIONS

1. C

A METAPHOR (Word 223) is a figure of speech comparing two unlike things. Director Zack Snyder compares Sparta to a "lonely citadel of freedom valiantly holding out against the tyrant Xerxes…" The correct answer is therefore C, "a vivid metaphor for heroic resistance."

2. D

IRONY (Word 226) is used to describe a situation in which things are not what they are said to be or what they seem. Mr. Williams criticized Alex for not fully exploring "the discrepancy between the literal meaning of what his protagonists said and what he really implied." Mr. Williams thus underscored Alex's failure to use dramatic irony. The correct answer is therefore D, "lack of dramatic irony."

3. A

The passage pinpoints "egregious flaws" in a movie that "should never have been filmed." Since the author's tone is harshly critical, the correct answer is A, "SCATHING" (Word 358).

4. B

The passage tells you that I.N. Stokes was a "dedicated reformer" who "fought against dumbbell tenements." Since "dedicated" supports "resolute" and "contended against" supports "opposition," the correct answer is B, "RESOLUTE (Word 352) opposition."

5. E

The passage tells you that Frederickson's "endlessly repeated clichés and slogans" bored the author. Since "clichés and slogans" are unoriginal and overused words, the correct answer is E, "TRITE" (Word 36).

6. D

The question asks you to find a first word that is consistent with "compromise" and a second word that is consistent with "force." Since compromise and force are antonyms, the answer must also be a pair of antonyms. The correct answer is CONSENSUS (Word 263) and COERCION (Word 267).

7. C

The question asks you to find a word meaning "triggering." The correct answer is CATALYST (Word 236).

8. A

The question asks you to find a word that describes the process by which people gain the right to vote. The correct answer is ENFRANCHISED (Word 266).

9. C

The question asks you to find a word that describes the misappropriation of funds. The correct answer is MALFEASANCE (Word 280).

10. B

The question asks you to find two logically connected actions that environmentalists committed to reducing global carbon dioxide emissions would advocate. The correct answer is ACCORDS (Word 256) and ARREST (Word 281). In other words, environmentalists want international agreements to halt the growth of carbon-burning factories.

11. E

The question asks you to find a word describing the effect "rugged natural obstacles" would have on an advanced trail. The correct answer is NEGOTIATE (Word 294) since these obstacles would make the trail difficult to hike.

12. E

The question asks you to find a first word that means "rigorously collected" and is the opposite of "abstract theories." The correct answer to the first blank is therefore EMPIRICAL (Word 242). The question then asks you to find a second word describing the impact Halle's EMPIRICALLY-based revolutionary conclusions would have upon the previous theoretical studies. The correct answer to the second blank is ECLIPSED (Word 288) since the new EMPIRICAL data made all previous studies "obsolete."

13. A

The question asks you to find a word describing the impact the "new polling data" would have upon the "once-upbeat" candidate. The correct answer is TEMPER (Word 295), since her falling popular support would force the candidate to TEMPER or moderate her "initial optimism."

14. D

The question asks you to find a word describing the creation of a new name or word. The correct answer is COIN (Word 289) since Ludacris is a coined or newly-devised name.

15. D

The question asks you to find a word that is consistent with President Kennedy's "great seriousness." The correct answer is GRAVITY (Word 282).

16. C

The question asks you to find a word describing characters who "were both formulaic and stereotyped." The correct answer is STOCK (Word 290).

17. B

The question asks you to find a word that is consistent with the key phrase "unconquerable female spirit." The correct answer is INDOMITABLE (Word 352).

18. A

The question asks you to find a pair of answers that are opposites since the people "alternate between contrasting temperaments." The correct answer is COMPLAISANT (Word 328) and PETULANT (Word 327). All of the other answer choices were pairs of synonyms.

19. C

The question asks you to find a first word that is consistent with "delivering speeches" and a second word that is consistent with being "learned and authoritative." The correct answer is ORATORY and MAGISTERIAL (Word 338).

20. E

The question asks you to find a first word that means "lied frequently" and a second word that means "great enthusiasm and flair." The correct answer is DUPLICITY (Word 318) and ÉLAN (Word 309).

21. A

The question asks you to find a word that means the opposite of "friendly and complaisant." The correct answer is PUGNACITY (Word 307).

THE UNIVERSITY CLUB

4/17/12

Marshall —

Would love to talk
to you about word
games on the site

Enjoy

Mark

PS Some great STEM
programs w/ Raytheon

22. C

The question asks you to find a word describing a "disgraced governor" who "was corrupt and easily bribed." The correct answer is VENAL (Word 314).

23. D

The question asks you to find a word that describes a songwriter who wrote so many songs that he had six #1 hits in one year. The correct answer is PROLIFIC (Word 372).

24. A

The question asks you to find a first word that means "surly" and a second word that means "arrogant." The correct answer is CHURLISH (Word 385) and SUPERCILIOUS (Word 395).

25. C

The question asks you to find a word that describes an artist who is "eccentric" and "highly individualistic." The correct answer is IDIOSYNCRATIC (Word 366).

26. E

The question asks you to find a word describing a host who provides "entertaining company, delicious food and a lively atmosphere." The correct answer is CONVIVIAL (Word 414).

27. B

The question asks you to find a first word that means "talkative" and a second word describing a "very different" person who is "guarded." The correct answer is GARRULOUS (Word 413) and TACITURN (Word 399).

28. B

The question asks you to find a word that is the opposite of "key figure" and is consistent with having "little influence." The correct answer is MARGINAL (Word 375).

29. E

The question asks you to find a word that means "variety." The correct answer is ECLECTIC (Word 391).

30. B

The question asks you to find a positive first word and a second word that is consistent with the phrase "mold it into almost any shape." The correct answer is EXTOLLED (Word 91) and PLASTICITY (Word 339). Note that in Choice D, while MALLEABILITY (Word 339) works for the second blank, DISPARAGED (Word 93) is a negative word that is not consistent with the key word "enthusiastically."

31. D

The question asks you to find a first word that means "impenetrably dense" and a second word that is consistent with "sophisticated." The correct answer is OPACITY (Word 312) and COSMOPOLITAN (Word 401).

32. E

The question asks you to find a word that is consistent with the key phrase "temporary expedient." The correct answer is STOPGAP (Word 383).

33. D

The question asks you to find a first word that is a synonym of "melodious" and a negative second word describing how "unfriendly critics" would view the influence of Markham's "jarring" music. The correct answer is EUPHONIOUS (Word 363) and PERNICIOUS (Word 410).

34. C

The question asks you to find a word that is consistent with the key phrase "an early warning." The correct answer is PORTENT (Word 323).

35. B

The question asks you to find a first word that is consistent with writing "voluminously" and a second word that means to maintain "exacting standards of research." The correct answer is PROLIFIC (Word 372) and METICULOUS (Word 8).

INDEX

WORD *Main Page*, Other Page(s)

A

ABSTRUSE *6*

ACCEDE *30*

ACCESSION *30*

ACCLAIMED *61*

ACCORD *21*

ACCORDS *21, 54, 121*

ACRIMONIOUS *26*

ADMONISHED *50*

ADROIT *74*

ADROITLY *54*

ADULTERATED *18*

AFFABLE *55, 62*

AFFLUENT *19, 72*

ALLUSION *1,* *10*

ALLUSIONS *10*

AMBIGUITIES *74*

AMELIORATE *27*

AMELIORATING *27*

AMIABLE *55, 97*

ANDECDOTE *67*

ANECDOTAL *8*

ANECDOTE *1, 8*

ANECDOTES *8, 66, 98*

ANTAGONISM *41*

ANTEBELLUM *48*

ANTITHESIS *20*

APHORISM *95*

APHORISMS *95*

APLOMB *49*

APOCRYPHAL *59*

APOPLECTIC *67*

APPEASE *22*

APPEASED *22*

APPEASEMENT *22*

ARCANE *83*

ARCHIPELAGO *28*

ARREST *34, 54, 121*

ARRESTED *89*

ASPECT *82*

ASTUTE *85*

AUTOCRAT *24, 25*

AUTOCRATIC *24*

AUTOCRATS *24*

AVARICE *18*

AVARICIOUS *38*

AXIOM *95*

B

BANE *63*

BEHEST *70*

BELEAGUER *54*

BELEAGUERED *54*

BELLATRIX *48*

BELLICOSE *48*

BELLIGERENT *47*

BENT *38*

BLATANTLY *31*

BLITHE *84*

CPSIA information can be obtained at www.ICGtesting.com
Printed in the USA
LVOW040926101211

258774LV00001B/5/P